PROTEST

IN THE LAND OF PLENTY

BY
AL CRESPO

CENTER LANE PRESS

DEDICATION

With love for my mother, Alice Crespo, who's interest and support made all the difference, and to Gina and George Ruffing, for always being in my corner.

IN MEMORY OF

Juliet Delgado
Mercedes "Chea" Pena

Copyright© Center Lane Press 2002
Copyright of all photos, Al Crespo
Copyright of all essays in this book remains with the individual authors of the essays

First published in the United States in 2002
By Center Lane Press

Library of Congress Cataloging-in-Publication Data
Crespo, Al

Protest In The Land Of Plenty/Al Crespo
p. cm
ISBN 0-9722134-0-6
Photography, Photojournalism, Protest, American History, 20th/21st Century

Title: Protest In The Land Of Plenty

This book was designed and laid out by Al Crespo
Text editing by Greg Corarito

Printed in Hong Kong
First printing, 2002

1 2 3 4 5 6 7 8 9 3/02

TABLE OF CONTENTS

FOREWARD
By Al Crespo

SECTION I: WHO'S VOTE? OUR VOTE
Essay by Adam Eidinger

SECTION II: THIS IS WHAT DEMOCRACY LOOKS LIKE
Essay by Nicholas Barricada
Essay by John Sellers

SECTION III: LIFE AND DEATH
Essay by Father Roy Bourgeois
Essay by Bruce Friedrich

SECTION IV: EXILES AT THE BARRICADES
Essay by Marleine Bastien

SECTION V: PROTESTS ACROSS AMERICA
Essay by Bob St. Louis

SECTION VI: THE COURAGE OF THEIR CONVICTIONS
Essay by Nate Madsen

FOREWARD

In May of 1997, on a trip to Argentina, I came across an incident which prompted the photo project which has led to this book. It was my last morning in Buenos Aires, and I was taking one last walk on the Avenida Callao, when above the cacophony of morning traffic I heard the sounds of protest. At the intersection of the Avenida Callao and Juan Peron, during the height of the morning rush hour, hundreds of high school students had come on to the street with banners and tires, and were mounting a protest in support of a hunger strike that teachers from throughout Argentina were staging several blocks away at the national Congress building.

During my time in Argentina, newspapers and television news shows had been full of stories of the hunger strike being waged by teachers throughout the country. I only had a small camera in my pocket when I came upon the student protesters, and I immediately started taking photos of these kids as they milled in the street, some with signs, others waving banners while attempting to rally the adults hurrying by on the sidewalks to work.

At first, against the din of car horns blaring, the rhythmic beat of drums and whistles that a handful of students were using as a way to provide a background rhythm to the event, I remained largely unnoticed, taking advantage of the general milling around by the students and passerby's to work my way around the edge as the growing surge of students began filling up the street.

As I started walking within the crowd of students, numbering perhaps 200, my photograph taking became noticeable, and some of the students began questioning who I was. On learning that I was

a North American, and accepting that I wasn't a police spy, some of the more outgoing students started asking me about what I thought of their protest, and whether students in the United States would ever protest like they were doing.

No, I replied. It had been a long, long time since I could recall high schools students going out into an American street to protest. And I could not recall students ever protesting in support of their teachers over any issue, especially over wages. This admission buoyed them. North American kids were obviously spoiled, one girl stated. Another bragged about how she and her friends were proud to be doing this in support of their teachers. At the same time their courage was fragile, and many made a point of covering their faces against possible recognition, even as they chanted their slogans.

High school students gather on the street in Buenos Aires to protest teacher salaries.

I stayed and talked with these kids for almost an hour. Once you got past the slogans and set dressing of protest, you realized that these weren't radical students intent on taking down a government, so much as they were impressionable children who had been influenced by the plight of their teachers, who in many instances made less than $200 a month.

On first sight, many of these kids had had a foreboding appearance as they milled around in the street with bandannas and ski masks covering their faces. The fear of retaliation by police and/or military is a reality in countries like Argentina, where recent history provided ample reason to hide your face if you chose to protest government action. Several asked me to take their photos and show them to North American kids as proof of their courage to stand up in protest against injustice.

These were somebody's 13, 14 or 15 year old sons and daughters, coltish, awkward and thoughtfully intense as they attempted to articulate what it was that they believed they would accomplish as passerby's hurried by and motorists blared horns, angered at having their morning commute disrupt ed.

In the weeks that followed, I would on occasion think about these children and the questions they raised about what North Americans - especially high school students - would feel so strongly about that they'd take to the streets in protest.

This led me to thinking about the nature of protest in America. Strikes and protest after all had long been the harbinger of momentous social change in our country. undertaken by our first radicals at the Boston Tea Party, to the massive labor protests before and after the turn of the 20th Century, American society had been molded by protest.

In addition, the impact of the civil rights and anti-war movements of the 60's and 70's with their massive marches, sit-ins and civil disobedience demonstrated the power of moral and ethical issues to galvanize hundreds of thousands of people to go into the streets in support of social change.

But now, as we came to the end of the century, I wondered whether Americans still viewed protest as a viable tool in implementing social change? Protest, it seemed, had become the domain of society's marginalized fringes. There appeared a palatable discomfort in the faces and attitudes of many Americans as they watched from the sidelines and tried to determine why, in the land of plenty that they believed America had become, would anybody still need to protest. For many of those with grievances, talk-radio served as the vehicle to vent their frustration.

In late 1997, I started taking my first photos of protests in Florida.

A student makes protest signs in the street.

These protests seemed on the edge of public consciousness and interest. Whether it was labor related, like the US Sugar workers strike in Clewiston, Florida, or protesters objecting to the launch of the Cassini nuclear rocket, the protests seemed not to connect with the public at large. Efforts to rally participation or the public's attention seemed to fall largely on deaf ears.

And so it was, until the World Trade Organization (WTO) arrived in Seattle for their annual meeting in November of 1999. During a period of 4 days, many Americans discovered that just beneath the placid surface, a new generation of protesters and protest groups had been organizing to deal with issues that were loosely identified as "globalization."

The WTO set new standards for protest participation. Instead of dozens, or hundreds of protesters, all of a sudden there were thousands. All of a sudden it seemed like a lot more people than anyone imagined were mad as hell and weren't going to take it any more.

Besides globalization, a lot of other issues suddenly captured America's attention. From police brutality to immigration issues, Americans were taking to the streets in large numbers.   In New York, it was the murder of Amadou Diallo and the attack on Abner Luiamia. In the South, especially South Carolina, it was arguments over the Confederate flag, a vestige of the Civil War. In Florida, there was the Saga of Elian Gonzalez, and the disparate treatment of Haitian boat people trying to reach America's shores. In Texas, more than any other state, it was the death penalty.

Out west, simmering arguments over land use led to the formation of the Jarbidge Shovel Brigade. The gauntlet they threw down in challenging the federal government. over a barely discernable strip of rocky trail that led nowhere revealed deep and longstanding hostilities by many in the west against federal agencies like the U.S. Forest Service.

And then there were the political protests. The Presidential election of 2000 provided a forum for protests unseen since the anti-war and civil rights protests of the late 60's and early 70's. The disputed votes in Florida led to new protests and resulted in hundreds of thousands of Americans, for the first time in American history, being subjected to metal detectors and searches before being allowed to watch a Presidential Inaugural parade.

Throughout the period that I traveled around the country photographing these protests, I was moved on numerous occasions by the humanity, sincerity and basic decency of average Americans, who, often facing ridicule, indifference, and on occasion the threat of violence or arrest accepted those challenges in order to stand up against injustice and the abuse of power.

On other occasions I came across "protesters" who had little if any understanding of the causes they were supposedly at the barricades to protest against, and who treated the process as little more than an opportunity to take part in what they considered the political version of extreme sports.

While this book captures many of the protests that resulted from the movement launched, in Seattle, my goal was to photograph the activities of all Americans with a grievance, be they to the left, the center, or the right of the political spectrum.

In the process, I, like many of my photo-journalist colleagues, managed to find ourselves under attack by both protesters and

A Los Angeles cop points shotgun at me seconds before I'm hit with rubber bullets.

police. For some strange reason, many of the loudest protesters advocating the "transparency" of government, and the rights of protesters to rampage through city streets as a way to drive their message home, were also the most vocal and physical antagonists against the 1st Amendment right of photographers trying to document these events. In all fairness, this problem at times was exacerbated by the infiltration by undercover police intent on using the cover of the news media to develop intelligence on the entire protest movement.

On the other hand, like many of my fellow photographers I managed to get tear-gassed, pepper sprayed and clubbed from one side of America to the other. Additionally, like a number of my colleagues I managed to get shot with rubber bullets while taking photos of Los Angeles police indiscriminately shooting at people on the streets around the Staples Center during the first night of theDemocratic Convention.

Yet, in spite of those occasional challenges, and even more so as a result of the threats to civil liberties now facing Americans as a result of the government's reaction to the events of September 11, 2001, I come away more convinced than when I started, that we need to cherish, support and even encourage the right of all Americans to stand up in protest as a right of citizenship.

Lastly, I wish to express my appreciation to the essay writers who took the time to share their experiences and opinions as part of this book. I suspect that not everyone will agree with some of their opinions, or solutions, to the problems that we face, but I hope that this opportunity to be exposed to their views provides Americans with a broader view of democracy in action as we enter the 21st Century.

- Al Crespo

BILL OF RIGHTS
ARTICLE I

Congress shall make no law respecting the establishment
of religion, or prohibiting the free exercise thereof; or abridging
the freedom of speech, or of the press; or the rights of the people
peaceably to assemble, and to petition the Government for a
redress of grievances.

WHO'S VOTE? OUR VOTE

THE REPUBLICAN CONVENTION

Over 10,000 protesters arrived in Philadelphia on July 30, 2000, determined to make their presence felt during the Republican Convention.

On Sunday, the first, and largest parade of the week, billed as the *Unity 2000 Rally*, featured a broad collection of groups and individuals paraded up the Benjamin Franklin Parkway in an almost festive street party atmosphere.

That was to change the following day when almost 3000 protesters gathered around City Hall, before setting off in defiance of police and city officials, who had denied the *Kensington Welfare Rights Union*, the parade's organizer's a permit to march.

On Tuesday, August 1st, protesters took to the streets in the early afternoon after police raided a puppet-making warehouse in West Philadelphia claiming that the facility held material to make bombs.

Starting sporadically, small bands of protesters engaged in a hit and run tactics, blocking an interstate entrance ramp to the north of downtown, and moving around the center of the city in increasingly larger groups until they eventually all but tied up traffic during afternoon rush hour.

Throughout the afternoon scuffles broke out between protesters and police, as some protesters attempted to set fire to dumpsters, and engage in other acts of vandalism. At one point, Philadelphia Police Chief Timoney, was himself attacked by several protesters who were quickly subdued and arrested.

Using horses and platoons of officers on bicycles, the police were able by early evening to regain control of the streets around City Hall. At the end of the day's confrontation over 400 protesters had been arrested, and the backbone of the protests were broken.

The *UNITY 2000 RALLY* got off to a festive start with giant puppets, and thousands of protesters, some of whom conveyed their message by dressing in costumes.

Below Right, Larry Holmes, one of the leaders of the *International Action Center* of Washington, D.C., leads marchers in a chant over the abolition of the death penalty.

Billionaires For Bush Or Gore, a group that maintained a constant presence at protests throughout the year 2000, attracted a sizable following during the Rally.

Supporters of Mumia Abu Jamal, America's most famous death row inmate staged a march through downtown streets on Sunday.

On Monday, John Varser and John Harker,(right), argued religion across from City Hall as protesters gathered around them waiting to see whether the city would grant a permit to the Kensington Welfare Rights Union.

An Anarchist supporter waves his flag during the Unity 2000 march on Sunday.

Masked protesters march through the streets of Philadelphia.

One way that the police dealt with protesters was with undercover police passing themselves off as protesters.

Defying threats of arrest, leaders of the Kensington Welfare Rights Union step off their march from City Hall to the Convention Center on Monday afternoon.

Police put out flag bunting set on fire by roving bands of protesters.

Locking their arms together, protesters sat in the streets awaiting arrest.

Former Philadelphia Mayor Rizzo's statute was a favorite target of paint bombs.

During one scuffle with protesters, police arrested everyone they could wrestle on the ground—including this volunteer medic.

This protester tries unsuccessfully to set fire to a dumpster. Moments later he was arrested by undercover cops.

By the end of Tuesday afternoon, downtown Philadelphia came to a standstill as protesters staged a massive sit-down around City Hall Plaza, which led to several hundred arrests.

THE DEMOCRATIC CONVENTION

As August 12th approached, expectations were high that protests during the Democratic Convention, would be marred by violence. Los Angeles Police, citing examples of street violence at the just ended Republican Convention, had called on city officials to bar access by the protesters anywhere near the convention site at the Staples Center in downtown Los Angeles.

Responding, the ACLU filed a lawsuit, and in what was considered a surprise move, U.S. District Judge Gary Feess, struck down the city's attempts to bar access by the protesters, as well as the city's permit procedures requiring a 40 day advance application and permit fees. In addition, the ACLU was successful in persuading the judge to bar the police from raiding or entering the D2K Convention Planning Coalition's Convergence Center.

Thousands of protesters, representing dozens of causes poured into the city the weekend before the convention, and on occasion found themselves matched almost person to person by thousands of police - many in riot gear - as they marched and gathered at the protest site across from the Staples Center.

On the first night of the convention, following a concert by the group *Rage Against The Machine*, police opened fire on hundreds of concertgoers with rubber bullets and bean bags, claiming that they were acting in response to rocks and bottles thrown at the Staples Center earlier in the evening.

The shootings failed to dampen the protesters resolve to continue their schedule of marches and demonstrations. Every day during the convention saw hundreds, and sometimes thousands of protesters staging events throughout the city. By week's end, 198 protesters were reported to have been arrested. In a final act of solidarity, groups of protesters camped out in front of the county jail vowing not to leave until their comrades had been released.

An LA police officer at the ready with a shotgun fitted to shoot beanbags

Like Philadelphia, marchers supporting Mumia Abu Jamal played a major part in the protests for the abolishment of Capitol Punishment in Los Angeles.

ROYALE
JEWELRY
PAWN
SHOP
A NEW WORLD?
HOW ABOUT...
FUN
SILLINESS
PEOPLE OF COLOR
IN LEADERSH
FREE

Protesters representing numerous causes march through LA streets.

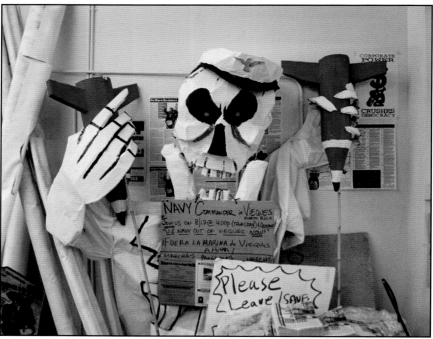

A federal judge's ruling prohibiting the police from trying to close the Convergence Center provide a safe space for puppeteers to prepare for the marches.

The Green Party came out in force to support Ralph Nader, their candidate for President.

As police move towards the crowd, a member of the Black Bloc reaches out towards a comrade laying in the street.

On Monday night, police opened fire indiscriminately on people in the streets around the Staples Center after closing down the concert by Rage Against The Machine.

Frightened by warnings from LA police and city leaders about the almost certain violence that would erupt in Los Angeles when the protesters arrived, shop owners were quick to lock themselves and their customers behind protective grates when protesters marched by. Here, a protest organizer tries to pass literature through the grate.

Ted Hayes, long time homeless advocate in Los Angeles, engages a member of the Black Bloc in an effort to avoid a confrontation with the police.. Below, members of the International Socialist Organization march with their capitalist pig.

A member of the Billionaires for Bush or Gore, cuts to the chase with her sign, during a mock press conference held by the Billionaires to outline their positions on issues affecting their members "financial" concerns.

George Clifton, who had been attacked by protesters a day earlier, expresses his opinion about Al Gore as protesters march by on their way to the Staples Center.

"VERMIN SUPREME 2000," a house painter/seasonal activist from Boston, who once ran for mayor of Baltimore, kept many amused with his rants and jibes at the police and their actions during the convention. He was at the forefront of many of the protests during both the Republican and Democratic Conventions.

Three days into the Democratic Convention, Los Angeles Police, according to Vermin, caught up with him on a side street and took his portable bullhorn. Above, Vermin walks the streets in a clear state of dejection after the seizure of his bullhorn. Later that day he managed to obtain another bullhorn, and once again got a spring in his step.

A protester wearing a mask of newly elected president of Mexico, Vicente Fox, leads a contingent of marchers during a march against U. S. immigration policies.

Morgan Stanley, Gore, Gray
Save ALL of Ballona Wetlands
International
Wages for Hous
Campaign
GORE

"OPEN THE DEBATES"

By Adam Eidinger

"**A** horse is not a weapon! A horse is not a weapon!" chant 2,000 people, who sit down in the entrance to the University of Massachusetts screaming and raising their fists. Their demand? Let Green Party candidate Ralph Nader in the Bush & Gore 2000 presidential debates. A cavalry of mounted riot cops walk their horses into this crowd; hooves break feet and bust heads. A nervous horse collapses, throwing its rider. The cop calvary retreats. They're going to have to negotiate with the demonstrators.

It all began in a Philly jail cell for me, one of 12,000 activists who converged in Boston for the first of three Bush-Gore tete-a-tetes. En route to an anti-death penalty protest, some undercover cops for the Philly MPD had arrested and jailed me for conspiracy. One subject of conversation that kept coming up during the eight days I spent in jail was the upcoming presidential debates. My cellmates and I were silenced in Philly, but if we could get Ralph Nader into the debates, we'd be vindicated.

Adam Eidinger, with bullhorn, leads protesters through downtown Boston.

Ralph's incisive, anti-corporate message could break up the corporate sponsored party duopoly, we agreed. Unlike Bush and Gore, Ralph spoke for us. This in mind, we formed the Open Debate Society (ODS) and vowed that upon release from our subterranean steel cell bloc in the Philly Roundhouse Jail, we would fight for Ralph's entry into the debates debates.

The first task of the ODS, an affinity group of D.C. Statehood Green Party members, students and democracy activists, was to

occupy and investigate 1200 New Hampshire Avenue, Suite 445, the only known address of the Commission on Presidential Debates (CPD). We found the address on their website and visited the building early in the morning September 20, 2000. Eight members of our group and a Washington Post reporter whom we had tipped off entered the building through a dry cleaner shop, using a back door to the lobby to avoid passing the security desk.

Once upstairs, we were surprised to find a tiny office marked with the names of two firms, Wagner Communications and the Brewer Consulting Group at the only known location of CPD. The two men we found inside first denied that the CPD was one of their projects. After we tripped over a box of pamphlets emblazoned with the CPD's official logo -- two birds with three wings between them (an apt depiction of the bipartisan venture), the men fessed up. Then they told us that if we wanted them to change the rules that exclude third party candidates we could put on our own debates.

Despite the misleading name, the "Commission" is not a government body. Nor is it a citizens' association like the League of Women Voters. It's a private non-profit corporation run by two political consulting firms, Wagner and Brewer, and funded by contributions from Anheuser-Busch, 3 Comm, and U.S. Airways.

The CPD puts on debates for Republicans and Democrats. If the Greens want to host a debate, "JUST DO IT," Mr. Wagner bellowed at us, comfy behind his sprawling desk.

O.K., Mr. Wagner, so all we need to do is figure out how to raise millions of dollars, how to get the corporate television outlets to air it, and how to get the major party candidates to show up, we bitterly responded. "Yeah, JUST DO IT!"

For about 45 minutes, my ODS companions and I systematically searched the CPD office. For art's sake, we also hung posters with slogans such as "CPD Corporate Puppet Debates," and blasted Beethoven's 7th Symphony on a huge radio. Eventually, the CPD had police escort us out of their office.

Protester uses Nader banner as gag.

A week later, the ODS made a second attempt to enter the CPD building. This time around, the cops arrested us and charged us with trespassing. "O.K," we decided, "if the CPD refused to be an open forum, we'll open it up using direct action!"

That's what brought the ODS to Boston, and we weren't alone. Two days before the first presidential debate, Ralph Nader held one of his super-rallies at the Fleet Center that attracted 13,000 supporters paying $10 dollars each, the largest paid political event of the 2000 campaign. At the rally, Nader talked about the upcoming debate and the CPD's role in preventing him and Pat Buchanan from participating. "To shut out legitimate third-party candidates from these debates is to limit the competitive democratic process on which the American electoral system is supposed to be built," Nader said, ending his speech with enthusiastic support for our planned protests. "I'll see you at the debates."

On October 2, 2000, the pro-democracy group "We the People" hosted a "Boston TV party" at the site of the original Boston Tea Party protest. The skillfully crafted public relations event featured supporters of third-party candidates in the presidential debates tossing TV's into the Boston Harbor (the TV's were tied to ropes).

The next day was the biggie, the date of the first presidential debate. Anti-corporate globalization activists began the day by marching around Boston's financial district and Harvard Square on "The Freedom for Sale Trail," a march planned by the Boston Area Mobilization (a grassroots umbrella organization that gave activists a forum to meet and work together on the debate protests) and sponsored by the Billionaires for Bush (or Gore). The Billionaires, an affinity group that showed up at the presidential conventions and other political events dressed up like aristocrats, yelled "More Poverty!" "Bush-Gore in 2000!" and left thank-you notes at each corporate office we visited. Approximately 1,000 people participated, halting traffic for nearly two hours; surprisingly, the police didn't arrest anyone. While stock traders and executive secretaries peered from the windows of glistening towers, the crowd blockaded Citibank, NationsBank, Chase, and Fidelity Investments, scolding each corporation for its anti-humanitarian misdeeds. While Chase, Nationsbank, Citibank all have questionable track record of lending money to corrupt, brutal political regimes, Fidelity holds Occidental Oil stock -- despite that company's assault on U'wa Indians in Colombia.

The protesters' message was that banking corporations have too

Marching to the tune of a different drummer.

much power over the lives of oppressed people worldwide. At the end of the Freedom for Sale Trail, members of the ODS met up with numerous other affinity groups, including the College Greens, at a metro stop near an auxiliary road to the debate site. A few hundred of us sat in the street, blocking police vehicles to disrupt their security apparatus. Suddenly, a large group of pro-Gore union members standing on the other side of a barricade began taunting us, chanting slurs. This was disappointing: Anti-corporate globalizationists had marched with unions in Seattle, Washington, D.C. and at the conventions to a lesser extent, but now we were on opposite sides of the protest. Riot police kept us apart.

"I thought labor was supposed to be on our side," I thought to myself. But union leaders like John Sweeney of the AFL-CIO and George Becker of the USWA had spent the election year telling their rank-and-file members to support Gore, the "lesser of two evils." This election opened my eyes to the weak leverage unions have in steering the political discourse when the candidate with the best credentials on their issues is shunned because he doesn't wear the Democratic label. After a couple of hours, my group marched away from the standoff and headed towards the main entrance to the debate site at U. Mass.

As we marched down the road, people marching from different directions joined our ranks. On the horizon we could see about 1,000 Gore supporters headed straight for us. Most were union carpenters who carried blazing orange and blue signs saying, "Gore is for Working Families." As the two crowds marched

Hundreds of carpenters march from union hall to the University of Massachusetts.

closer to one another, some people in our group became nervous.

We were out numbered, and these union guys were big! Though we chanted "Union! Union! Union!" and sang "Solidarity Forever," the air thickened with tension. As we passed the offices of the Boston Globe, we met the Gore-supporting unionists. I was in the front of the pro-Nader march. The carpenters pushed us to the side of the road. One screaming Gore supporter grabbed a cross out of the hands of a School of the Americas protester and summarily whacked it over his head. The protester bled while scores of other carpenters grabbed and hustled the assailant away. Later I heard the same carpenter attacked a Nader supporter and was arrested by police. Some union guys sheepishly told me that the assailant had a little too much to drink at the union hall.

By the time we reached the main entrance, it was dusk. Our march joined at least 1,000 other open debate supporters who stood along the road, watching as reporters and guests invited to the presidential debates were bussed in to the debate hall. Laura Jones, Nader's press secretary, called me to say that Nader had gotten a ticket and was going to try to sit inside the debate hall. Shortly before dark, the crowd spotted Nader on a bus heading into the debate. He waved and the mostly college-age crowd screamed excitedly, "Let Ralph Debate."

By dark, the pro-Nader crowd had grown to at least 9,000. Anti-death penalty and pro-Palestinian marchers arrived in the thousands because they felt there was no real difference between

Bush and Gore on their issues. The union/Gore crowd had shrunk to a few hundred. Members of the anarchist Black Bloc numbered in the hundreds and scuffled with police along the barricades at the eastern end of the "protest pit," a designated area by the police for "lawful dissent."

Protesters grabbed the Gore/Lieberman signs tied to barricades along the road and defaced them. The Democrats, oversized, 8 x 3 foot signs had been posted everywhere, but not for long. In an interesting twist, scores of union members put down their Gore signs and joined the open debate protest. In unison, we chanted "Al Gore, Chicken Debater, He'll Debate George Bush but not Ralph Nader!"

At 9:00 P.M. my cell phone rang. It was Laura Jones again. She explained in an angry voice that after two attempts to enter the debate press reception area, Nader had been accosted by CPD officials who threatened to arrest him if he did not leave the campus immediately. An armed group of riot police confronted him.

Police try to keep protesters from breaking out of protest area.

Nader left in disgust, vowing to sue for discrimination since he had a valid ticket.

After I got off the phone I announced over a bullhorn that there was news from Ralph Nader. About 500 people in the area I immediately stopped chanting and formed a circle to listen. I explained what Laura had told me and then talked about why I came to Boston. "If you really believe in what we are trying to do, you would be willing to lay your life down for democracy," I said. I urged the crowd to join me by the waterfront for a brief spokes council to plan a direct action to open the debate going on inside.

In just a few minutes about 500 people formed a circle on a hillside near the water. Protesters who saw a large mass moving within the crowd joined in the spokes council, passing bullhorns. My job was to enforce a loose form of consensus process and to "take stack," slang for keeping a list of who wants to speak.

Very quickly our group decided to take the street connecting the campus, which sits on a peninsula, to the mainland. The plan was simple: Fifty people willing to risk arrest volunteered and moved to the center of the spokes council circle. We passed a sign-in sheet to get names and nick-names, and to make sure no one would be left in jail.

The remainder of the group was asked to give as much money as they could afford for a bail fund and to spread along the barricades. The generous crowd passed thousands of dollars to the center of the circle. The 50 volunteers each received between $50 and $100 to cover possible fines. After a half-hour the spokes council broke up, and the core group of "arrestables" walked in a line four-wide. The column walked together, arms locked, chanting "open the debates," towards the barricades; I stood just 20 feet away. Black Bloc anarchists and other affinity groups spread out all along the quarter-mile of metal barricades that separated 9,000 or more people from the street and about 400 black clad riot cops standing on the opposing hillside.

This was it. A great scream went up from the crowd and everyone began to push the barricades. In just a few seconds thousands of pounds of metal flipped over like a house of cards. The "arrestables" rushed out into the street. Initially the police didn't react and the "Black Bloc" followed in behind the group tearing at the barricades, breaking them into small sections and rearranging them so they blocked the street. The "arrestables" were sitting on a meridian spread out on both sides of the street. Soon, police on horses moved in and attempted to push the "arrestables" back. Some "Black Bloc" people took the barricades and used them to round up the police horses. This tactic worked at first and a stalemate ensued for about an hour. Police kept creeping up on

Black Bloc members start breaking up the barricades.

us as more protesters took to the street. In all about 2,000 sat in the street, trapping the people inside the debate hall.

The riot police used clubs, pepper spray and hard plastic shields against people sitting close to the reinforced phalanx. A few officers grabbed some of us, and a tug-of-war ensued. In two hours, the police arrested 12 people for blocking traffic and disorderly conduct.

Eventually the commanding officer on duty stepped forward

and asked us if we would negotiate. By now it was clear that the police didn't want to arrest 1,000 of us, or even 100 of us. They were under orders, it seemed, to show restraint. It would be very embarrassing if there was a mass arrests at the debates. People nationwide might start asking "why?"

After about one hour of negotiations with the police - led by members of the Boston Area Mobilization (BAM) - the protesters agreed to leave the premises upon release of people in custody, including the union thugs who attacked us earlier.

Eventually, the police produced six of our people held in custody on site, but the remaining arrestees had already been taken to the police station. The commanding officer told us that as long as there were no outstanding warrants, everyone would be released by 6 a.m. the next day. Our group, still sitting in the streets, arms still locked together, stood up and marched away, chanting "Solidarity Forever."

As we marched away I felt euphoria and exhaustion. We had achieved a victory of sorts. Our dissent was militant and peaceful. We hadn't opened the debate, but we did transform our dissent into an extreme confrontation that played out in newspapers and on television worldwide.

Were the debates a display of Democracy in America? We didn't think so. The real democracy that day happened in the street.

THE POST ELECTION PROTESTS

Americans woke up on November 8th, 2000, to learn that for the first time in over 100 years, the election of the President and Vice President was in dispute. It didn't take long for the world to find out that the problems seemed to be located in Florida.

Within days, partisan Democrats and Republicans protesters hit the streets in West Palm Beach, a most improbable place for political protests to erupt, as claims were made that the now infamous "Butterfly Ballot," used in Palm Beach County had caused thousands of elderly voters to cast their votes for the wrong candidate.

Protests then spread south to Fort Lauderdale and Miami, and then north to the state capitol in Tallahassee, as lawyers carried their fight over the disputed ballots to the State Supreme Court.

From there, the legal battle and protests went north to the U.S. Supreme Court in Washington, D.C., where on December 12th, the United States Supreme Court issued their controversial ruling which ended the legal wrangling over the counting of the ballots, and made George W. Bush the 43rd President of the United States.

Gore supporters were the first to gather outside the Palm Beach County Courthouse to voice their displeasure with the count.

Not everyone in West Palm Beach was happy to see Reverend Jesse Jackson show up.

A protester with a lot to say.

Cuban exiles in Miami try to rally motorists for Bush.

Denise Lorenzo, a Gore supporter, stands her ground in West Palm Beach.

Reverend Jesse Jackson leads a protest march in West Palm Beach over the contested ballots.

Republican protesters in Fort Lauderdale came out in large numbers to protest the absentee ballots of the military being disqualified.

While lawyers for George Bush and Al Gore argued their case inside, Angeline the Polka Queen, and her partner, King Ira, of Gainesville, entertained the protesters and news media gathered outside of the Florida Supreme Court building.

-38-

Whenever a TV camera appeared, demonstrators supporting Bush or Gore would push and shove in the hopes of getting their opinion on the air.

David LeGrande, argues with an unidentified Bush supporter in front of the U.S. Supreme Court.

Reverend Jesse Jackson, flanked by Rabbi Stephen Jacobs of Los Angeles, and Patricia Ireland, president of the National Organization of Women,(NOW), lead a march of approximately a thousand demonstrators past the U.S. Supreme Court while the legal debate took place inside.

Reverend Al Sharpton, Reverend Walter Fauntroy, and Marion Barry, former mayor of Washington, D.C., join other protesters in front of the U.S. Supreme Court.

On a cold and rainy January 21, 2001, George W. Bush was sworn in as the 43rd President of the United States, and made his way from the U. S. Capitol to the White House under the most intense security ever provided a U.S. President on his Inauguration.

THE IMPEACHMENT OF PRESIDENT CLINTON

On the morning of December 19, 1999, as the U. S. House of Representatives took up the Articles Of Impeachment against President William Jefferson Clinton, approximately 700 members of the news media gathered on the grounds east of the Capitol to chronicle this historic event.

Several hundred spectators, many who had begun lining up before dawn, stood at the South entrance of the Capitol waiting for the opportunity to sit in the visitors gallery and witness for a few minutes, history being made.

On the Capitol grounds, mingling among the press were curious onlookers. At the edge of this growing crowd, gathered a small collection of protesters. They were conspicuous by their paucity. At the most, the number of people who had come to protest for or against the impeachment numbered no more than several hundred people at any one time throughout the day.

Some came with homemade signs, others bought materials and made their signs while kneeling on the ground. Several bought American flags. For the most part they stood in silence as onlookers and occasionally photographers and reporters wandered over to look at their signs, or ask why they had felt the need to show up and protest.

The crowd, even though it grew in mid-afternoon to approximately 4000, largely remained silent, gathering around individuals who had bought portable radios to listen to the debate inside the House chambers.

By the end of the day, the House of Representatives had voted to support 4 Articles of Impeachment, making President Clinton, only the second President, and the first since 1867 to be impeached by the House of Representatives.

As protesters and on-lookers gathered across from the U.S. Capitol, they stood silently around radios, listening as the impeachment debate took place inside..

Supporters of impeachment gathered across from the U.S. Capitol break into cheers at 1:19 P.M., as news is broadcast over the radio that the House of Representatives had just cast it's first impeachment vote against President Clinton.

Standing alone with her flag, this woman came to the Capitol to express her opposition to the Impeachment of President Clinton.

Pro and anti-impeachment protesters gathered in front of the White House to express their opinions after the House had completed it's impeachment vote.

William Mann, a carpenter from Fredericksburg, Virginia, marches in front of the White House shortly after the impeachment vote.

THIS IS WHAT DEMOCRACY LOOKS LIKE

THE WTO

In the short period of time which has passed since the WTO protests took place during the last days of November, 1999, in Seattle, Washington, it is evident that momentous changes have occurred within the protest movement and in the public's awareness surrounding the issues that have become known as globalization and world trade.

Prompted by a myriad of issues and concerns involving the often secret governmental policies which have led to globalization of trade through organizations such as the World Trade Organization (WTO), tens of thousands of people - for the first time since the Vietnam War - came onto American streets to protest government policies. Seattle provided a matrix for heretofore incompatible groups such as labor unions, issue organizations and "radical" groups and individuals to work together in furthering agendas that they discovered were not mutually exclusive.

The protesters in Seattle also emboldened the representatives of smaller nations to stand up within the WTO to protest what they considered domination by the larger industrial powers, including the United States.

For most people, the lasting impression of the WTO were the acts of sporadic property damage inflicted by small, roving bands of protesters intent on attacking what they believed to be symbols of corporate greed.

The larger, and more lasting impressions of the WTO protests however, centered around the ability of protesters to seize the attention of the world and focus it on the impact that organizations such as the WTO and other global governance institutions have had, largely in secret - in becoming the shapers and custodians of a world economy.

Demonstrators march to protest the actions of the Seattle police in attacking demonstrators with teargas and night sticks.

Marchers by the thousands thronged Seattle streets to voice their concerns about the WTO.

Protesters jeer police above, while other protesters dressed as Turtles were a colorful addition to the marches and rallies.

Masks became a standard part of protest attire at the WTO.

Organized labor put thousands of their members onto the streets of Seattle to demonstrate against the labor practices of multi-national corporations in the 3rd World.

Native American protesters turned out in force to support environmental concerns and the release of Leonard Peltier, a member of the Anishinabe Nation, considered by Amnesty International to be a "political prisoner," who should be released immediately.

The Seattle Lesbian Avengers march against the WTO.

On the last day of protest a protester circles a group of motorcycle police with sticks of incense in a healing ritual.

THE BLACK BLOC

By Nicolas Barricada

Over the years the term "black bloc" has been associated (usually thanks to the stellar reporting of the mainstream media) with anything from indiscriminate hooliganism to highly organized "gangs" that infiltrate peaceful protests with the sole intention of attacking police, as well as with every other slander in between.

As a result of this widespread misinformation it seems almost impossible to begin to discuss what exactly black blocs are, what they do, who they are composed of, how they function, and most importantly, why it is that they exist and are likely to continue existing for quite some time, without first making clear what they are certainly not.

Black blocs are not a formal organization. One cannot be a "member of the black bloc". Likewise, black blocs did not originate in Seattle or Washington DC (as is often reported in the press) and have indeed existed since much before the "Battle of Seattle."

Black blocs do not have leaders (not Colin Clyde, not Jaggi Singh) and we are not all influenced by the primitivist ideas of John Zerzan. Indeed, it is only a small fraction of black bloc participants that identify with primitivism. Above all, it is probably most important to note that, while people who participate in black blocs believe that it is legitimate to use revolutionary violence and tactics deemed "illegal" in order to resist and confront capitalism and the state (whether it be by fighting police, damaging property, or whatever other means), this does not necessarily mean that a black bloc is always violent, or that it exists for those sole purposes.

Black Blocs originated in the 80's in Germany, as a tactic emanating from the Autonome and Anti-Fascist movement. The German Autonome movement was (and still is) a movement that had as its principle focuses of struggle in those conflicts which could simultaneously both undermine the state and build a class conscious fighting culture, hence building up the working class resistance movement by creating a culture of resistance centered on autonomous struggles, free from the influence of opportunist political parties or corrupt trade unions. This was aimed at reaching an eventual crossroads of autonomous and revolutionary struggles and achieve an eventual total rupture with capitalism and the state. To build the new society in the shell of the old.

As a result of this it entered into frequent conflict with the state (defending squats, fighting fascists, blocking nuclear transports, etc.) hence having to deal with a relatively high degree of violence and repression.

It was for these reasons that they began to wear masks in order to hide their identities, as well as helmets and body armor for protection, as well as batons and other such street fighting weapons for offensive actions (such as attempting to break police lines or fighting fascists). Furthermore, in order to make their section of the demonstration tighter and more difficult to disperse (as well as for propaganda purposes) they lined the front and side with banners and poles. Inside the "bloc" it was expected that everyone be part of a line, composed only of people who knew and trusted each other, and that lines of people who were acquainted with each other be together forming a "cluster," thus

Nicolas Barricada

providing for greater tactical fluidity and confidence, as well as making police infiltration more difficult. This is the basic organization of what the German police began to term as the "black bloc," a term that the German Autonomes and Anti-Fascists originally rejected.

Since then, black blocs have spread throughout Europe and across the ocean to North America. Black bloc tactics are still most commonly seen in countries with strong radical autonomous fighting cultures, such as Italy, Denmark, Sweden, Greece, and of course, Germany (although it is now illegal in Germany to wear a mask at a demonstration), among others, but they have begun to be adopted to varying degrees all across Europe and North America.

Although black blocs originally emerged to serve a very precise function, that of militant attack or defense in mass conflict situations, they have now come to serve a broader

Keeping an eye on the police at the A 16, IMF/World Bank protests.

purpose for revolutionary anti-authoritarians, particularly anarchists (who now make up the majority of people participating in black blocs). The reasons for "masking up" at a demonstration, aside from defending oneself against police identification and possible repression, are many.

It is often the case that anarchists are only seen as anarchists by others when engaging in illegal actions or masked up in a black bloc. The fact is that this is not true, as anarchists engage in a

variety of struggles and embrace many different tactics. At mobilizations, while anarchists are certainly present in the black bloc, they are also medics, cooks, non-violent civil disobedience participants, and everything else. However, this aspect is often ignored. As a result, anarchists have on occasion masked up, not in order to engage in militant actions, but in order to assert their presence at a mobilization and not allow themselves to be counted merely as more foot soldiers for one political party or another, as well as to dispel misconceptions about anarchism.

Two prominent examples of this would be the anarchist Black Bloc at the Philadelphia Millions for Mumia march in 1999, which numbered in the thousands and was completely peaceful, and the "Trash Bloc" at the border action in Buffalo during the FTAA summit which, after claims by the media and police that the anarchists would "trash the city" went around the city picking up trash in impoverished areas.

The black bloc is also used as a means of expressing solidarity, both practically and symbolically. Practically, we express solidarity, for example, by refusing to allow the forces of the state to take any of us without a fight. Hence, black blocs attempt to perform "de-arrests." This literally means taking people who are being arrested away from the hands of the police. Of course, being accustomed to the usually timid and guilt ridden protest culture that glorifies arrest, police officers are often quite shocked by this, making successful de-arrests easier. In addition, black blocs often come to the aide of non-violent protestors who are coming under attack from police. This was the case at the World Bank mobilization in Washington on April 16th, 2000 where the bloc of approximately 1000 people was dedicated primarily to supporting those engaged in non-violent actions by drawing police away from them.

The symbolic solidarity of black blocs lies in that by all dressing alike and marching together, we are all at equal risk of police repression, regardless of who does what. Thus, the more timid people in the larger bloc play a part in the action by providing a body of cover for those engaging in direct action to retreat into. Thus, one expresses solidarity by implying that it does not matter who exactly it was that broke the window or attacked the police line, "it might as well have been me; it was all of us."

Furthermore, there is an unfortunate tendency in the media to trivialize resistance movements which threaten the establishment. This is usually done by focusing more on the people who are in the movement, than the message itself. Thus, by looking alike and concealing our identities, we are saying that who we are is not important. Despite the media's insistence that we are all angst-ridden teenagers, we come from all walks of life. We could be high school students, university stu-

dents, unemployed, squatters, part time workers, nurses, doctors, construction workers, white, black, Asian, young, old and everything in between. What is important is not so much who we are, but what it is that we have to say.

Yet another use of "black blocs," especially in North America, is to empower people by showing them that the roads that the state gives us to "protest" are not the only ones available and that we have power much stronger than the false voice of the ballot. This is the power of the people, the power of our creativity, and the power of direct action.

By not being under the control of any party or reformist organization we become truly autonomous and free to develop our struggles and our visions for a New World. We open the doors to glimpse what a different world, a participatory and egalitarian world based on the principles of direct democracy, self-management, decentralization and mutual aid might look like, and just how powerful that vision is. By conducting and organizing ourselves, and our "black blocs", in such a manner, we show people what that world might look and feel like, and that is a powerful sight.

Finally, and possibly most importantly, ""black blocs"" serve to add a militant tone to otherwise tame and compromising situations. They serve to radicalize fellow demonstrators as

Crashing through barricades in Washington, D.C., during the Bush Inauguration.

well as to add a revolutionary and insurrectionary dimension to what might otherwise be just another demonstration to forget. The fact is that we are revolutionaries, not hard-edged reformists, as some seem to think.

We are interested in nothing less than the total destruction of capitalism and the state and the creation of a classless, stateless society to replace it. To us the only relevant goal of our movement and our demonstrations should be to advance the struggle against capitalism and the state, to build a revolutionary movement that satisfies itself with nothing less, and to eventually effect relevant social change in the benefit of the oppressed of this world, not by covering up the wounds of capitalism with reforms, but by completely changing the dynamics and structure of our world. Not as a vanguard or as leaders, but as fellow fighters in one common struggle.

Because of all this, we aim to see every demonstration filled with potentially insurrectionary scenarios. Creating free zones where police cannot enter, distributing or free the necessities of life, allowing people to take freely the commodities that otherwise serve o enslave, urging workers to strike actively and take back their workplaces from their exploiters, forming open general assemblies to serve as the decision making entities in communities, attacking the temples and physical representations of capitalism and the state, and much, much more.

Evidently, when coming from this perspective, conflict with the

repressive arms of the state is inevitable, and to us it is essential, in order to be more effective in our struggle, to be well organized and well prepared for it. The black bloc, as a tactic, while far from perfect and only one tool in an arsenal that includes everyday work in communities and workplaces, propaganda through books, newspapers, and magazines, and much more, is certainly an important tool in this respect. It is the street-fighting element of a movement that is, by definition and necessity, combative.

As our movement grows and our struggle intensifies, so does the degree of repression from the state and its abilities to counter the black bloc tactic. Hence, it is becoming time for us to continue working to make it eve more effective. As new people start participating, we need to make i clear to them that a black bloc is not a free for all and that there is an important degree o discipline, commitment and responsibility necessary for participation in a black bloc.

Yet, even more importantly, we need to become effective no only as a force on the streets, but as one par of a culture of resistance that, while implicated in all the relevant social struggles of our time, maintains its independence by never forgetting that the state has an astounding ability to adapt to and absorb partial attacks, thus remaining fundamentally unchallenged by reformism. It is up to us to create an anti-authoritarian movement of uncompromising resistance that is not subject to the ups and downs of the particular issues of the day, but instead fights on until total victory. Once we have created this movement and this culture, it will truly be time to begin creating "the New World in the shell of the old."

Black Bloc members marching in Los Angeles.

A 16 - IMF/WORLD BANK PROTEST

In the aftermath of the WTO protests in Seattle, the police in Washington D.C., prepared for the expected protests against the IMF/World Bank meetings in April of 2000, as if a marauding army of Huns had announced plans to invade the nation's capitol.

A fifty block section around the World Bank Headquarters was quadrangled off in an attempt to deny protesters any opportunity to get close enough to disrupt the arrival and departure of the attendees.

In addition, believing that the best defense is an offense, the police on the Friday night, before the weekend actions began, hemmed up about 300 protesters who had been staging a peaceful march and arrested many of them.

The police also raided the Coordinating Committee's Convergence Center in Northwest Washington and closed it as a way to disrupt the protesters ability to organize. And finally, to further nullify the efforts of the protesters, the delegates to the meetings were ferried to the meeting site in bus convoys very early in the morning.

Though tens of thousands of protesters had been expected, and while approximately 10,000 took part in a Sunday march, only 5000 or so took part in efforts to block the streets leading to the World Bank Headquarters. On the last day, several hundred protesters - after several hours of negotiation - were allowed to cross the barricades in front of the bank's headquarters in a symbolic act of civil disobedience before being arrested.

Protesters gathered at sunrise on the first morning to block the streets leading to the World Bank.

Puppet makers have made an important contribution to getting the protester's messages across with these large puppets.

"She hit me!" he cried out, as police tried to order photographers not to take pictures as they unsuccessfully attempted to break up the protesters blocking a street.

Black Bloc members charge down 14th Street towards a waiting line of police. Below, police deal with the aftermath of the charge, and stop 2 young men for questioning.

One of the first protesters arrested on Friday night before the beginning of the scheduled protests . These arrests were a move by D.C. police to arrest as many of the protesters as possible, thereby creating gaps in the leadership within the ranks of protest organizers.

The protesters principal strategy was to block all of the streets leading to the World Bank building.

Louise Rameriz, a member of the Gray Panthers shows that you're never to old to hit the streets for a cause.

Waiting for the other side to do something is often the primary strategy between protesters and police.

Supporters of Mumia Abu Jamal march in front of the U.S. Justice Department as part of a protest against the prison industrial complex.

One of several scuffles police had with members of the Black Bloc on the 2nd day of protest.

On the last day of protest, after several confrontations with police while attempting to breach the barricades a block from World Bank headquarters, an agreement was reached allowing those protesters wishing to engage in civil disobedience to cross the barricades, 10 at a time, and be arrested. Many of those sitting down here were waiting for their opportunity to be arrested.

THE RUCKUS SOCIETY

By John Sellers

The Ruckus Society provides activists with the tools they need to build power and win. We aid and abet a number of different organizations and movements in the effective use of nonviolent tactics and strategies. Ruckus was founded in 1995 to build skills and capacity within the forest movement. Since that time our program has evolved to support a wide array of environmental issues as well as struggles for human rights, social justice, and organized labor. Because the thread of unchecked corporate audacity weaves it's way through all these issues we focus much of our attention on stemming the tide of corporate globalization.

Of course corporate globalization is just a fancy new description for something that's been around for thousands of years: Greed. However, it is only in the last five hundred years that humankind (men actually,) have managed to elevate systemic forms of greed to a global level. Whether you call it feudalism, empire, colonialism, imperialism, global capitalism, or corporate globalization it appears to be the same ugly bunch of old white bald dudes that have been running this planet and it's human population into the ground for the better part of recorded history. Any CEO demonstrating a comparable track record in the corporations that we're up against would have been fired long ago.

Unfortunately for everyone involved, these captains of industry and their good friends who run the planets governments are running out of real estate. Their history of greed has finally brought us to the brink of systemic failure. Fortunately, they are also running out of excuses. As globalization has made the planet smaller and smaller, it has allowed for the emergence of a truly glob-

al civil society. This has in turn given rise to an extraordinary community of non-governmental organizations struggling for a more ecologically sustainable, socially equitable, and politically democratic future for the children of Earth. Ruckus exists to serve these institutions in their struggle.

We occupy a unique niche in the political landscape, simultaneously exhibiting attributes of networks, alliances, and organizations. Institutionally we are very small. Our staff, of just 5 full time employees, works (almost on top of one another,) in an office in Oakland, California, not much larger than a conventional phone booth. However, orbiting around the paid staff are concentric rings of experienced trainers, facilitators, coordinators, and logistics specialists that comprise the 'Ruckatista' community. There

John Sellers

are now around 150 of these 'Ruckatista' volunteers all over North America from a diverse array of organizations and campaigns. This is where our real strength lies.

We like to think of ourselves as a kind of virtual volunteer fire department for the movement. Our goal is to hold a place in the center where different struggles intersect. Whether you are standing in the path of deforestation, battling against sweat-shops, or the expansion of the private prison industry you need the tools and training to carry on an open and public debate. You need to create powerful and inspiring symbols that will pierce through the dissonance and inspire ordinary folks to throw themselves into the gears of the machine. Ruckus attracts practitioners of creative nonviolence from a diversity of backgrounds with a track record of proven effectiveness in nonviolently taking down "the Man".(taking on the fight for global justice.)

The centerpiece of our program is Action Camp. We bring 100 - 200 activists together in a beautiful outdoor setting for a week-long, dynamic skill share. Participants spend their days steeped in a wide array of theoretical and applied workshops. In the evening they are treated to plenaries, panel discussions and cultural events.

Ruckus core curriculum includes but is not limited to the following: Strategic Campaigning & Action Planning, Strategy Media & Communications Training, Nonviolence Philosophy &Technique, Internet/Digital Activism and Lobbying, Political Theater, Banner Construction & Rigging, Blockades & Support Roles, Action Climbing Techniques, Anti-Racist Organizing, Grassroots Organizing, Direct Action Imagery and Legal Considerations for Direct Action.

The objective is to provide an opportunity for participants to hone effective strategies and tactics, develop leadership skills, pass technical expertise onto a new generation of activists and party like rock stars. Ruckus has a demonstrated commitment to confronting the uptight, self-righteous, gloom and doom activist stereotype head on.

Attendees get lessons in climbing. Some go on to hanging banners from buildings and bridges.

How can we appeal to the public if we don't look like we're more fun to be around than the corporate clones on the other side of the fence?

We now have close to 3000 alumni of the Ruckus program working for virtually every just cause that you can imagine. It's an incredible feeling to bear witness to the inspiring actions that they have helped to create all over this continent and increasingly all over the world. It is thanks to their sacrifice, imagination, and hard work that the notoriety of Ruckus has spread far and wide. The media and the authorities have given us far too much credit, or blame depending on how you look at it - witness the $1 million dollar bounty on my head at the Republican National Convention in Philadelphia - for the resurgence of non-violent social struggle here in America.

We're happy to play some small role in supporting ordinary folks taking extraordinary risks on the front lines. They follow in the footsteps of the African American citizens of Montgomery, Alabama, who refused to ride on racist buses and turned the tide against segregation. They are descendants of the yippies and young people that ended the US war against Vietnam. They channel the courage of suffragettes who would not yield until American women were enfranchised with the vote. They are the farmers from India and British housewives that have halted Monsanto's biotech juggernaut. They stand in solidarity with the Zapatistas and indigenous struggles of self- determination everywhere. And they are now the worldwide movement of movements that stands in the path of the hostile corporate takeover of our planet.

Hopefully some of these frontline heroes and sheroes will someday tell their grandchildren about how the struggle for global justice was won. By then kids will probably take their diverse, democratic and sustainable international civilization for granted. Maybe some of those crotchety old grandparents will remember the first time they went skinny dipping at that crazy Ruckus Action Camp. How they met other visionary activists who would become their life-long friends. How they received 3 square gourmet Vegan meals a day and all the training they could cram into their hungry brains. Maybe they'll smile when they remember conspiring around the campfire to build a more just society. I hope so.

Learning how to make protest posters and signs to get the message out.

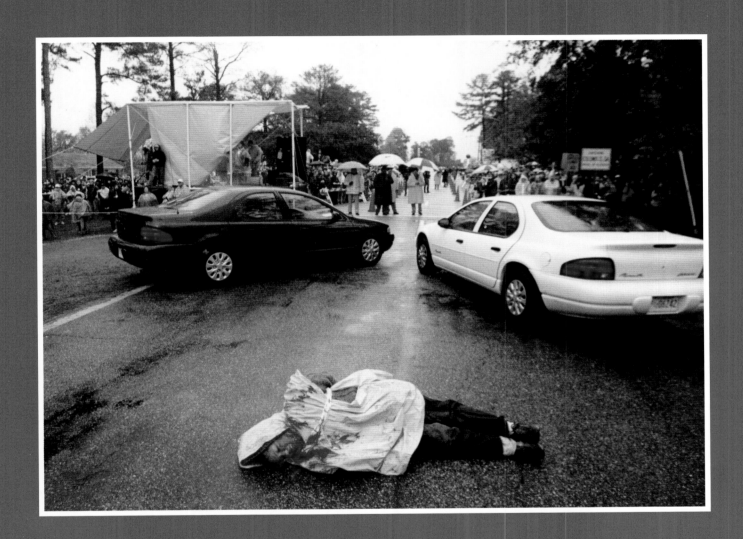

LIFE AND DEATH

Sister Helen PreJean addresses an anti-death penalty rally on the steps of the Ohio State Capitol in Columbus, Ohio.

THE EXECUTION OF GARY GRAHAM

On June 22, 2000, a very hot and humid day in southern Texas, approximately 750 protesters gathered outside the walls of the state prison in Huntsville to protest the impending execution of Gary Graham.

Graham, who admitted to a crime spree which had included a series of violent armed robberies as a teenager, had steadfastly continued to proclaim his innocence of the murder that had put him on Death Row, even as the protesters gathered.

Most who came to Huntsville that afternoon, came to protest against Graham's execution. Others, including a dozen or so members of a Cleveland, Texas branch of the Klu Klux Klan came to celebrate his impending death.

The increasing evidence of deep flaws in the way that the death penalty is applied across the U.S., has given impetus to a burgeoning movement determined to abolish - or at least slow down - the application of the death penalty in America. Growing numbers of protesters now routinely show up at prisons across the country to bear witness to their opposition of what they believe is murder by the state.

In Texas, on that hot June day, the occasion provided an opportunity not so much for thoughtful debate, as for street theater by the Klu Klux Klan and the New Black Panther Party, and for a lingering question to remain after the deed was done: Had an innocent man been executed.

Protesters march through Huntsville towards the prison.

Skip Davis,(left) argues with Klan members about the execution.

Protesters rallied outside of the Huntsville prison where speakers addressed the crowd, and prison officials watched in wary anticipation from behind a barricade as everyone waited for the time of execution to arrive.

Reverend Jesse Jackson and Bianca Jagger talk with the press before going into the prison to witness Graham's execution.

Members of the New Black Panther Party from Houston, Texas, march through the streets around the prison with their guns. Texas is a state which allows citizens to carry

Approximately a dozen members of the White Camelia Knights of the Klu Klux Klan came to protest for Graham's execution.

Momo Motapa, of Houston, Texas, engages in some ritualistic chanting while the crowd behind him watches an American flag burn.

THE SCHOOL OF THE AMERICAS WATCH

By Father Roy Bourgeois

We've all experienced suffering in this world, and much of the suffering we can't do much about. But there's another kind of suffering, a suffering brought about by greed, violence, militarism and foreign policy. This kind of suffering we can address. We can relieve it. We can confront it and change it.

The School of the Americas in Fort Benning, Georgia, has caused and continues to cause a lot of suffering among our sisters and brothers in Latin America. This is not a complicated issue; it's about men with guns. It's about violence. It's about the poor.

The starting point is not this school at Ft. Benning. It's Latin America where the vast majority of our sisters and brothers struggle for survival. They live on the edge in their shacks without running water, they are not paid just wages for their labor, they do not have schools for their children, and so many of the children are dying before their time. It's out of this struggle, this suffering, that their people will come to our country to learn how to be commandos.

In the 1960s I spent four years in the military and thought seriously of making the military a career. When they asked for volunteers to go to Vietnam to fight the communists, I didn't question the generals. The suffering there, the violence and the death, changed me. Losing friends, being wounded, I was forced to look at my faith more seriously, ask questions I had never asked before.

I think in our lives there is this mysterious divine grace at work, calling us to be more human, to be more compassionate. I left Vietnam and entered the seminary. All I knew was that somehow I wanted to be a healer, wanted to work with the poor. I was ordained a Catholic priest and assigned to Bolivia as a missionary. I have come to believe that we are called to be peacemakers in our world. To work for justice, to be healers as best we can where we are.

The people were so good, sharing what little that they had with me, welcoming me into their homes. They became my teachers; those I went to serve, taught me. They taught me about my country's foreign policy in their country. It saddened me to see we were supporting a brutal dictator, General Hugo Banzer, who had come into power through a violent coup; one of the many dictators to rule Bolivia. They taught me about the CIA, so active throughout Latin America at that time. They taught me about the multi-national corporations arriving in their countries; the new conquistadors that arrive with their suits and briefcases because there are huge profits to be made on the country's vast resources and off the backs of the poor.

Father Roy Bourgeois, at the Republican Convention in Philadelphia.

But most of all, they taught me a new theology. They introduced to me their struggle for liberation, for peace, for justice, for food for the table. The poor of Latin America have been taught a very cruel theology. They were told, and many of us were weaned on this theology, to accept their suffering as God's will, to embrace their lot in life, and look forward to joy in the next life. How cruel to blame all of this on the Creator.

Today, that is changing. They've come to discover a living God, a Creator who does not want them to suffer. But rather One who is calling them to liberate themselves from poverty and oppression. And they are saying, "Basta! Enough! We are not going to sit back and suffer in silence anymore."

I felt blessed to be a part of that struggle. For the first time, I was seeing history through the underside, through the eyes of the poor. I was very happy as we went about our work, building a clinic, starting a literacy program, a daycare center. In my fifth year I was arrested for speaking out against the oppression and forced out of Bolivia. I came home very sad, but I felt a responsibility to talk about what I'd seen and heard.

In 1980, in El Salvador, Archbishop Oscar Romero was gunned down at the altar for his defense of the poor. That same year, four U.S. church women, three Catholic nuns and a lay worker, were raped and killed by the Salvadoran military. What was going on throughout Latin America could be seen in El Salvador. The elite, living so well in their mansions with live-in servants and shopping sprees to the U.S. and Europe, had on their side the men with the guns. And what angered us as North Americans was to see those guns arriving from the U.S.

I came home from El Salvador and I spoke out. When 525 Salvadorians arrived at Ft. Benning to begin combat training here on U.S. soil, I said, "Basta!" "Enough!" It could not be business as usual. I left the comfort of the pulpit and the security of the classroom and went to Georgia.

In Columbus, Georgia, home of Ft. Benning, with 25,000 active-duty army personnel, I found a little house and invited friends to come. Our resistance community grew in number. Then it come time for us to take our message to the Salvadoran soldiers on Ft. Benning. Three of us, Linda Ventimiglia], who was in the Army Reserves, Larry Rosebaugh, who had worked with the poor in Brazil for years, and I went to an army surplus store and bought army uniforms.

We dressed as high ranking army officers and went to Fort Benning that night, carrying a powerful boom box that contained the last sermon of Archbishop Romero; the one he gave in the cathedral in San Salvador the day before he was assassinated. In that sermon he made a special plea to the men in the military saying, "Stop the killing! Cese La Opresion! Stop the oppression.!Lay down your arms, disobey your superiors telling you to kill your fellow compesinos, your fellow brothers and sisters, and obey a higher law, that law that says thou shall not kill." He was killed the next day.

We wanted to take Bishop Romero's words one more time to the Salvadorians now in U.S. barracks. We penetrated the high security area and used tree climbers to scale a tall pine near the barracks. About 30 feet up, we secured the boom box and waited. When the last lights went out, we said, "Bishop Romero, this is for you, brother," and his voice boomed into the barracks. It was a sacred moment. Those soldiers came out of the barracks, young men looking into the sky and hearing the words of this prophet. Instructors ran out with their M16s, spotted us in the tree, and threatened to shoot us down. We left the box up there, blasting away. We were charged with criminal trespassing and impersonating officers, and after we were convicted we were sent to different prisons for 18 months.

Prison was hard, but we learned something very important. They can send us to prison, but they cannot silence us; truth cannot be silenced. We spoke from prison and when we got out of prison, we spoke louder than

Protesters came from all over America. Their messages were often simple and direct.

Protesters wearing "death masks" and carrying the coffins symbolizing he many murdered peasants lead the protesters onto Ft Benning.

before, joining thousands of people around the country, trying to stop the military aid to El Salvador. But the military aid, up to $1 million a day, and the bloodshed continued.

November 16, 1989, another massacre. At the university in San Salvador, past midnight, six catholic priests of the Jesuit order, their co-worker, a young mother, and her 15-year-old daughter Selena, dragged out of their rooms and killed. A congressional task force reported that those responsible were trained at the U.S. Army's School of the Americas.

I headed back to Georgia to find out what the School of the Americas was all about. I invited friends to join me. We had work to do. We started a water-only fast, camping out at the main gate of Ft. Benning. It was hard but we took it one day at a time, trying to call attention to this injustice.

Our bodies grew weak, but our spirit was strong. We lost a lot of weight during those 37 days. Every day people would come with their guitars and their poetry, their hope, their energy. It was wonderful. It sustained us.

Through the Freedom of Information Act and human rights reports coming out of Latin America, we began to piece together the history of the school and its graduates. The school began in Panama in 1946 to bring stability to Latin America. The U.S. Army, financed by U.S. taxpayers, trained over 50,000 soldiers from all over Latin America. Perhaps their intentions were noble, but something went wrong. Dictators went through the school, death squad leaders like Robert D'Aubuisson from El Salvador and General Manual Noriega. General Hugo Banzer, is not only a graduate from Bolivia, but in 1988 he was inducted into the school's hall of fame where today his photograph hangs with some 20 other generals presented as model soldiers.

In 1984, the school was forced out of Panama, and quietly settled at Fort Benning where today it is operating full force, training between 1,000 and 1,500 soldiers from all over Latin America. This is not a Peace Corp oper-

for over 900 men, women and children killed at El Mosote, 10 of them went through this school. But it wasn't only El Salvador. In May 2000 , a human rights report came out of Guatemala outlining the genocide of the indigenous Mayan people. The report said over 200,000 Mayans were killed and many of the killers had been trained at the School of the Americas.

They came by the thousands, average Americans, came to bear witness and risk arrest.

ation; it's a combat school. Soldiers learn how to be commandos with psychological warfare, sniper training and counter insurgency techniques. The question we ask is, who are the insurgents? They are who they have always been. They are the poor and those who dare to accompany the poor in their struggle. University leaders, human rights advocates, labor leaders, church leaders and health care worker have all been the targets of soldiers who learned their lessons at this school.

In 1993 the United Nations' Truth Commission Report on El Salvador was made public. We learned that in the case of Bishop Romero, of the three responsible for his death, two of them trained at the school. The rape and murder of the four church women - of the five responsible, three of them graduates. The two women and the six Jesuits - of the 26 responsible, 19 of them went through that school. Of the 12 responsible

In September of 1996, the Pentagon was forced to announce that at this school, from 1982 to 1991, there were manuals used that advocated torture. This got the attention of a lot of members of congress when it hit the front page of the Washington Post and the New York Times.

We knew that if we brought this information to the public people would pay attention to this kind of suffering. People of good will, people of faith, began to respond.

The Presbyterian Church at its annual assembly in 1993 passed a resolution with its 5.8 million members calling for the school's closing. It was the first national organization to come on board and that influenced other faith communities. Right after them, Veterans for Peace, a national organization, came on board, saying that this school is bringing shame upon our country. Next the leadership conference of Women in Religion with 97,000 Catholic nuns came on board.

Thousands of letters began to arrive in Washington while many groups, Amnesty International, NAACP, and more recently, AFL-CIO with its 13 million members came out with resolutions saying the school should be closed. And I'm happy to say 150 U.S. Catholic bishops joined the group. They should have been the very first to come on board. What were they waiting for? It's sad to see our shepherds becoming government sheep.

People are saying to their leaders, "You better speak out on this." And they're not waiting for the leaders; they are speaking, they are moving. Editorials appeared in major newspapers around the country. The Chicago Tribune printed an editorial, "Lights out at the School of the Americas." The New York Times printed a strong editorial, the second actually, calling for its closure, titled, "School of the Dictators." The Boston Globe called it, "The School of the Assassins."

In 1993, Representative Joseph Kennedy from Massachusetts introduced a bill calling for the close of the

It was a cold and rainy day as protesters gathered in front of the gates at Fort Benning.

school. It lost by a vote of 174 to 56. Every year we go to Washington and fast. In 1994, on the steps of the Capitol, a group of us conducted a juice-only fast for 40 days. People come from all over the country. And every year, just about, that vote would narrow to a close. Last year for the first time we got enough votes to cut off a big chunk of the funding. Then it went to a Senate conference committee where it lost by one vote. But we are not to be discouraged.

What's important is to keep our hands on the plow; our eyes on the

prize. To keep the spirit of the movement strong, to keep it energized. We gather at the main gate of Ft. Benning. We started way back in 1990 on the first anniversary of the massacre of the two women and the Jesuits. We had 10 people there that first anniversary. The next year, 100 came. And the next year, 300 came. Then, two years ago, something happened; 2,000 came. Every year we have a memorial service, speakers and some good music to uplift the spirit. The memorial service keeps alive the memory of our sisters and brothers in Latin America and what's happened to them. We use our voices for them; those who have been silenced.

At Ft. Benning they have drawn a white line across the road and say if we cross that line, we are trespassing. When we gather their every year we ask, "What law are you talking about? A law that protects this training that leads to suffering and death in Latin America? There is a higher law; the law of conscience, the law of our hearts, the law of our faith that says, 'No! We are to be healers. We are to be in solidarity with the poor here at home and elsewhere. And that's the law that we are going to follow today.'

We cross that line in a solemn funeral procession, carrying coffins with the names of the victims. Over the microphone, the names are called. "Ita Ford," one of the church women. Everyone in unison answers, "Presente! She is here with us today." "Oscar Romero" and everyone answers, Presente! He is here with us today. " They stopped our group of over 500 that crossed the line a few years ago and found that 25 of us were repeat offenders who had crossed the line the year before. They indicted us, brought us to trial, charged us with criminal trespassing. Included in our group of 25, in the courtroom facing Judge Elliot once again, was Sister Rita Steinhaven, a 71-year-old nun from

Minneapolis. Before our sentencing, each of us spoke from the heart about why we did what we did. I'll never forget a Jesuit priest from Tacoma, Washington, Bill Bichsel, who said, "Your honor, you can send us to prison, but you cannot silence us. We will speak from prison. You cannot kill this movement. We are going to come out of prison and we're going to come back here every year in greater numbers." We each received a six month prison term and $3,000 fine.

During my time in prison, I began to question what we were doing, but something happened and I was brought to my knees. I think it was one of those moments of grace. It came through the words of Dorothy Day, this wonderful woman who started many soup kitchens and houses of hospitality for the poor, the homeless. She said, I remember so well her words, that we are to concentrate on being faithful, and not worry too much about being effective. Let's do what is in our hearts. Let's be faithful to that, not knowing how that is going to have any kind of effect but knowing it will bear fruit. Perhaps not immediately, but it will not be in vain.

That was liberating. I felt free in that cell. So free that I got out of there in good shape as each of us did. We came together, a big reunion, just in time to start organizing for November.

But the big question was, would people come back to Georgia? Would they come knowing that they could get arrested and sent to prison? Oh, did they come. From all over the country, 7,000 came and 2,000 crossed the line. And then, this past November, something incredible happened. They came in greater numbers. Twelve thousand gathered at the main gate.

Twelve thousand! Incredible. Right after the memorial service, 4,408 people crossed the line. They've just indicted 23 of our group and they are awaiting trial. They too speak from prison and they too energize this movement.

The movement is strong; but we need the voices of others. We are up against a giant here. The Pentagon is fighting hard to keep this school going. It's their way of controlling Latin America. You control a country's military, you control their people. They are talking about changing the name of the school perhaps, a little window dressing at the school, maybe relocating it to some other place. We say, no, no, no. This will not work. We are not going away. We are not going away.

I think Archbishop Oscar Romero has a big message for us. Before he was assassinated, he said, "Let those with a voice speak for the voiceless." We have a voice, you and I. May we speak clearly and boldly on this issue and all the other issues of peace and justice.

Martin Sheen, actor and long time activist, kneels with other protesters on the road inside Ft. Benning while waiting for military police to process them and issue warnings not to trespass again or face arrest.

A father pauses with his son, as they look down on one of the protesters assuming the role of a murdered Latin American peasant.

THE KILLING OF AMADOU DIALLO

The issue of police brutality has been the basis for protests through much of American history. In recent years police brutality has been viewed as a serious and reccurring problem in a number of American cities including New York. In the late 1990's, the city witnessed a series of high profile murders and assaults by police on minority citizens, including the murder of Amadou Diallo, a west African immigrant, in the vestibule of his Bronx apartment house, who died in a hail of 41 bullets while reaching for his wallet.

The death of Amadou Diallo, served to galvanize many New Yorkers into questioning the actions of police in New York City when it came to policing in minority neighborhoods.. Led by the Reverend Al Sharpton, a series of months long protests resulted in the arrest and trial of the 4 policemen involved in Diallo's death.

In January of 2000, the policemen went to trial in Albany, the upstate state capitol of New York state. On February 25, 2000, a jury returned a verdict of "Not Guilty," against the 4 officers, prompting a major protest in New York City the following day .

Approximately 5000 protesters, starting at the park across from the Plaza Hotel on 5th Avenue and 59th Street, marched throughout lower Manhattan, in the process engaging in sporadic acts of civil disobedience by lying in the street and blocking traffic. By the end of the evening, when they reached City Hall several dozen protesters had been arrested.

The vestibule where Amadou Diallo was gunned down.

Police read their rights to protesters staging a sit-down on 5th Avenue across from Saint Patrick's Cathedral before they are arrested, handcuffed and taken away.

"It's a wallet, not a gun!," chanted protesters as they marched down 5th Avenue.

RIGHT TO LIFE

Every January since 1974, hundreds of thousands of Americans have traveled to Washington D.C., to take part in the annual *March For Life*, to protest against *Roe v. Wade*, the U.S. Supreme Court decision which legalized abortion on demand.

Gathering at the Ellipse on the Mall, protesters take part in a rally before setting off on a march to the Supreme Court, where they pray and sing hymns. In 2001, on the day after the inauguration of President George W. Bush, over 250,000 marchers gathered on a cold and clear day to take part in this annual march.

This is just one of an ongoing number of events, including picketing abortion clinics, trying to persuade women who visit abortion clinics not to go through with the procedure, and on several occasions murdering health care workers at abortion clinics that members of the pro-life movement have undertaken in support their contention that abortion should be outlawed.

On an earlier occasion in 2000, across the country in Los Angeles, members of the *Right To Life* movement, seizing on the media coverage surrounding the Democratic Convention in August of 2000, staged several events including picketing an abortion clinic in South Central Los Angeles.

The battle over abortion shows no signs of waning, and is now considered a cornerstone of political and social activism for many Americans.

Right To Life members march in the parking lot next to Staples Center, in Los Angeles.

Right To Life protesters used media coverage surrounding the Democratic Convention to call attention to their cause by staging a press conference in front of the Staples Center on the Sunday before the convention began. They then carried out several actions, including one at an abortion clinic in South Central Los Angeles, above, where they were met by pro-abortion demonstrators.

Right To Life member holds up signs to demonstrate the choices between abortion and life.

March For Life participants lined up across Constitution Avenue as they marched towards the U.S. Supreme Court.

Some of the 250,000 plus marchers at the 2000 March For Life.

Demonstrators came from all over America to take part in the march.

January 22, 2000, was the 28th anniversary of Roe vs. Wade, the United States Supreme Court decision which allowed abortion on demand. Every year since the court issued it's opinion, there has been a rally and march held in Washington organized by the March To Life committee as a way to show opposition to the Court's opinion.

Daniel Martino protests against abortion in front of the U. S. Supreme Court on May 15, 2000

By Bruce Friedrich

As long as humanity continues to be the ruthless destroyer of other beings, we will never know health or peace. For as long as people massacre animals, they will kill each other. Indeed, he who sows the seed of murder and pain cannot reap joy and love.

-Pythagoras

People for the Ethical Treatment of Animals (PETA) was founded in 1980 with the charter statement, "Animals are not here for human beings to eat, wear, experiment on, or use for human amusement." PETA is now the world's largest animal rights organization, with more than 700,000 members.

Since PETA's inception, we have been devoted to grassroots activism, including using demonstrations, leafleting, street theater, and civil disobedience, as a means of reaching people and creating a societal discussion of animal abuse. If you make your demonstration interesting enough, you can reach not just the people you see, but also the people who see you on the news or in the paper.

As just a few examples, in our vegan campaign, we go to schools with activists dressed in cow costumes to pass out "Milk Suckers" trading cards (see MilkSucks.com) that parody the garbage pail kids from the mid-1980's and alert children to the fact that consuming milk supports the veal industry and leads to obesity, acne, allergies, and other illnesses; at meat trade shows, it often happens that someone in a pig costume will show up at the convention hotel and unload a dump truck full of manure (the truck has huge "MeatStinks.com" banners emblazoned

along the sides); and every year, when the American Meat Institute hosts its "Congressional Hot Dog Lunch," we bring our "Lettuce Ladies" (Playboy Playmates) to serve Veggie Dogs and talk about the fact that eating meat contributes to impotence.

Slaughterhouses are perhaps the most violent places on the planet. Cows and pigs are routinely sent kicking and screaming through the skinning and dismemberment process, and chickens and turkeys are routinely boiled alive in the feather-removal scalding tank, every one bleeding, suffering, and dying exactly as they would if they were human beings.

Farms today treat animals like so many boxes in a warehouse, chopping off beaks and tails and genitals with no painkillers at all, inflicting third degree burns (branding), ripping out teeth

Bruce Friedrich

and hunks of flesh. These are Frankenstein animals, genetically manipulated and pumped full of hormones. Chickens, as one example, develop 6-to-7 times as quickly as they would naturally, so that their hearts, lungs, and legs often give out under the pressure.

Animals transported to slaughter routinely die from the heat or the cold, or freeze to the sides of the transport trucks or to the bottom in their own excrement. Dairy cows and egg laying hens endure the same living nightmare as those who are raised for their flesh, except that their time on the so-called farm is longer. They are still shipped to the slaughterhouse and killed at a fraction of their natural life span.

There is simply no excuse for anyone who considers themselves to be an ethical human being, let alone an "animal lover," to be supporting such practices, all of which are routine and universal throughout the industries which turn animals into meat products. If you are eating meat, you are supporting the grotesque abuse of animals.

Every time any of us sits down to eat, we make a decision about who we are: Do we want to add to the level of violence, misery, and bloodshed in the world? Or, do we want to make compassionate and merciful choices? There is so much violence, from war torn regions of Africa and Europe, to our own inner cities and right onto our dinner plates. Most of this violence is difficult to understand, let alone influence. Veganism is one area in where each one of us can make a difference, every time we eat.

The question then becomes: How do we communicate this to a public jaded by tabloid television and sensationalized news? PETA has found that we can often reach people most successfully when we begin with humor or something interesting and different: It is very difficult to get angry with a Playboy Playmate or with someone dressed up as Jesus or a pink fuzzy pig. After the laughter or the gawking, comes debate.

At PETA, we see our goal as educational, letting the public know, for example, that if you look into how cellophane-wrapped meat makes its way to the grocery store, and have even a modicum of compassion within you, you will be horrified. To that end, we speak in colleges, send out press releases, and utilize Internet-based activism on a massive scale.

PETA turns up wherever people are discussing issues of morality, issues of life and death, or almost any issues at all:

PETA pigs at the Republican Convention.

For example, a pro-life march is the perfect place for a discussion of the anti-life stance involved in meat eating.

The Southern Baptist Convention, held in Orlando in May of 2000, where Christ (the Prince of Peace) is celebrated, was the perfect place to talk with people about the hell on earth that is today's factory farm and slaughterhouse, and about the denial of God involved in treating God's beloved animals like so much dirt.

And political conventions are excellent places to bring the message that eating meat adds to our nation's healthcare costs due to sick days lost and insurance costs, and that raising animals for food is environmentally catastrophic, depleting ground water and wasting crop resources as well as squandering land and polluting waterways.

As politicians discuss budget priorities, we address the fact that adopting a vegetarian diet is the best choice for human health, for the environment, and for the animals. And of course, there are more than 10,000 media representatives at the conventions, many of them tired of covering the same boring speeches.

Basically, if there is a group of people interested in discussing issues, we will try to be on hand to let people know that animals are feeling, thinking beings, and that they value their lives much as we value ours.

A PETA member, dressed as Jesus, stands in front of the Orange County Convention Center in Orlando, Florida, trying to persuade passerby's to go vegetarian.

MILLION MOM MARCH

On Mother's Day, 2000, an estimated 750,000 mothers (and fathers), gathered on the National Mall in Washington D.C.., to send what they hoped was a powerful message to the members of Congress regarding gun control, and the need to pass legislation to register all handguns.

The march was the idea of Donna Dees-Thomases, from New Jersey, who got the idea for the march after watching reports on television about a shooting in a New Jersey day camp.

The issue of gun violence, including the murder of hundreds of children annually, has long been a rallying point for those opposed to gun ownership in America.

The Million Mom March prompted one of the largest gatherings in Washington in recent memory, and provided an opportunity for many who had been personally affected by gun violence to express their pain and commitment to seeing stronger gun controls enacted.

A sign which summed up the position of many at the Million Mom March.

The Talley family displays their reason for supporting gun control. There were dozens and dozens of families from across America who also came to the rally as the result of the murder of a family member.

Labor Secretary Alexis M Herman, and First Lady Hillary Clinton, led off the march which took place on the Mall before the speeches began.

The National Rifle Association and their opposition to new gun control measures, was the target of many protest signs.

Not everyone in Washington that weekend supported gun control. Counter-protesters affiliated with the Sisters of the 2nd Amendment, a group who supports gun ownership staged their own rally and march from the Mall to the U.S. Capitol..

EXILES AT THE BARRICDES

LOS VAN VAN

In October of 1999, Los Van Van, a wildly popular Cuban musical group on a tour of American cities, came to Miami for a performance at the Miami Arena.

In response, several thousand Cuban exiles turned out to protest the group's appearance. For years, Anti-Castro Cuban exiles had maintained a hard-line opposition to the appearance in Miami of any Cuban musicians or artists. On at least one occasion, a museum was bombed where Cuban art work was shown.

Protesters, who outnumbered the concert-goers by a wide margin, staged a loud and angry protest, exchanging insults with some concertgoers as they arrived. Concertgoers returned the fervor with their own taunts at the protesters. As the concert began, few protesters chose to leave, waiting instead in the streets across from the arena for the concert to end.

As the concertgoers left, many under police protection, protesters began throwing Coke cans, eggs and bottles of water. The night ended with 10 protesters and 1 concertgoer arrested.

In the aftermath, the actions of the protesters that night were seen by some as a dress rehearsal for the months of protests that followed the arrival on an innertube of the little Cuban boy Elian Gonzalez who washed ashore the following month.

Anti-Castro Cubans rail against concertgoers as they entered the arena.

A Cuban exile protester waves a noose, indicating what he'd like to do to the concertgoers.

Giving the finger seemed to be the favorite form of expression among many protesters on both sides of the barricades.

HAITIANS IN AMERICA: AGAINST ALL ODDS

By Marleine Bastien, LCSW

Although Haiti became the first black republic and the second nation in the Western Hemisphere to achieve complete independence and the only nation to abolish slavery, the "civilized" world never accepted Haiti's independence. Efforts to free themselves and change their society were constantly threatened by imperial interests of the Vatican, France, and the United States, who waited more than half a century to recognize Haiti.

After Haitians paid a heavy indemnity to their tormentors, France recognized the new government in 1838 Throughout the 19th century, a small mulatto elite battled with the black masses for control, while outside powers plotted to reintroduce slavery and to restore Haiti to its colonial status. The United States ignored Haiti until President Abraham Lincoln recognized it during the U.S. civil war.

Marleine Bastien at a protest rally in Miami.

As a result, for much the 19th century, Haiti was isolated from the rest of the world. During this time of isolation, Haiti developed the basis for its contemporary class structure and political traditions. An elitist neocolonialist society was selected over the introduction of mass education and other developments that would have raised the standard of living and met the needs of the majority poor. The elitist model generated many internal conflicts that led to constant instability.

In 1915, during World War 1, President Woodrow Wilson sent U.S. Marines to Haiti in a preemptive move against the Germans, who were showing increased interest in Haiti. The goal of the American occupation, which lasted until 1934 was to oust the Europeans and convert the Haitian economy to U.S. needs. In the guise of maintaining political stability, the control of economic resources was placed in the hands of a tiny minority who were allied to foreign investors and a National Guard was trained according to U.S. standards to protect U.S. interests rather than to defend the black Haitians.

The U.S. occupation of Haiti laid the groundwork for the development of a series of authoritarian, oppressive regimes that would guarantee political stability by keeping the majority of Haitians in poverty, continued repression and political submission.

One of these regimes, the dictatorships of Francois Duvalier,(1957-1971) and his son, Jean-Claude Duvalier,(1971-1986) used the bloodiest forms of repression, and state terrorism against the Haitian people. Consequently, thousands took to the sea, in non-seaworthy vessels in an attempt to make the 750 mile voyage to Miami. These fragile boats defy the imagination and speak to the desperation and the tenacity of the refugees who resigned themselves to live or die at sea. Many did die. Only the sea can tell the stories of these hopeless refugees who made the decision to make the ill-fated trip to the land of the free...the land of the free?

The Haitian presence in the United States is not new. Haitians have immigrated to the United States since the American Revolution. Many Haitian nationals have made significant contributions to American culture. For example, Jean Baptiste Pointe de Sable built the first permanent settlements for what is now known as Chicago.

Almost one thousand Haitians fought against the British in the battle of Savannah in 1779. Haitians were viewed more as a curiosity than a nuisance; the image of Black men speaking French was quite a nouveaute. The U.S. only started to really take notice when the Haitians began to come en masse in the late 1970s.

Protesting in front of U. S. Coast Guard Station in Miami.

Haitians began to experience difficulties when they reached critical mass. The fear was that this "sea" of Haitian immigrants would be contributing to the "browning of America." The decision was made then to stop the boat people at all costs.

The policies that came from this decision resulted in U.S. agencies such as the Immigration and Naturalization Service and the U.S. Coast Guard to detain and deport Haitians refugees as fast as possible, with complete disregard of their rights. Ignored in the process was the fact that many would face horrible death upon return in Haiti.

The first wave of refugees came primarily because of direct political oppression during the first decade of the rule of Francois Duvalier, (1957-1967) who eliminated all opponents, real or perceived.

The second wave of refugees consisted of skilled craftsmen who came to the United States looking for better living conditions owing to economic hardships. After the death of Francois Duvalier in 1971, the replacement by his son Jean-Claude Duvalier, led to continued political repression and the waste of natural resources.

The third wave of Haitian refugees consisted of peasants who had been dispossessed of their land or were unable to make a living on the deteriorated soil. These immigrants came in 1980, around the time of the Cuban exodus from Mariel.

The fourth wave of immigrants came in 1991, after the coup d'e tat that overthrew now Haitian President Jean-Bertrand Aristide. These refugees were mainly young students, member of grassroots organizations, peasants, women, and human rights activists.

Haitian's by the thousands would gather after work to protest, many bringing their kids.

It was during the third wave of Haitian boat people arriving on the shores of South Florida, that U. S. administrations undertook a policy of trying to return them as soon possible to Haiti with a complete denial of their most basic right: the right to due process. These administrations have contended that although a few Haitians deserve asylum, the vast majority were economic and not political refugees .

According the U.S. authorities, "allowing the mass of boat people to remain in the U.S. would establish a precedent which would make it impossible to deny access to other economic refugees," such as those from Mexico and other parts of Latin America and the Caribbean .

The U.S. government's consistent denial of full, fair hearings for the Haitian boat people was racist, biased, and illegal under international and U.S. law because the United States has a nondiscriminatory, binding commitment to protect refugees from persecution.

The INS's policy, vis-à-vis the refugees, was to detain them and arbitrarily deport as fast as possible. Consequently, the refugees were herded in the courtrooms so quickly - sometimes 10 hearings were conducted at the same time - that refugees had two hearings in front of different judges the same morning. The aim of the speed up process was INS's attempt to expeditiously deport the refugees without a fair chance to request political asylum.

A group of Haitians incarcerated at Fort Allen, Puerto Rico for months, sent an open letter to the INS out of sheer desperation to appeal to their sense of humanity. "Since 1957, we have

Children are often separated from their parents by the INS.

endured atrocious suffering due to the lack of a good government...but now it is worse, and we cannot stand it. This is why we are forced to emigrate in larger numbers. At home, if we manage to get work, we cannot collect our salary. If we claim our rights, our life would be in danger. Not only one's own, but also that of the entire family, which would be implicated by the authorities.

"To our great surprise, upon arriving to the Immigration Detention Center in Miami, we were made to wait for hours during which time we were interrogated on one single topic, to wit, "Why did you come to the United States?" Upon arriving, our eyes widened with fear and surprise at the treatment and condition of life. We thought we were throwing ourselves into a stable. One thousand persons jammed into the same cell. It reminds us of black slavery, but alas, after shedding many tears and imploring God to come help us, we finally resigned ourselves to accepting this sufferance....because we did not want to go back.

"Since we arrived on American soil, we have been mistreated. We have been made to suffer and we have accepted it all, we have endured it. How can we return to Haiti now?, empty handed and stripped of everything? Oh no, it would be the greatest injustice. If the Americans did not want to take us in, they should have sent us to other countries like Russia, Cuba, France or Canada that are willing to take us in with open arms? We are Christians. We have blood in our veins and thoughts like all other people who are free. We want our freedom because we have been suffering for five months , because we left our relatives in order to help others get out of the lion's mouth in Haiti. Our situation is pitiful. We have been locked up behind barbed wire from Miami to Puerto Rico. The days are always the same for us. We don't know what the date is. Sometimes we are hungry and cannot eat. We have needs and cannot satisfy them. Is this the better life we are seeking? We took refuge in the United States in the hopes of filling our voids. Can we not fill them? Where are we going? Now we cannot stand it any more. It is too much. If we have not been freed by the end of November, a good number of us are going to commit suicide. Because we have sworn to die in the United States..."

These practices were current even during one of the worst and bloodiest dictatorship the world has ever known, that of Francois Duvalier, (Papa Doc), and his son Jean-Claude Duvalier, (Baby Doc), and after the military coup d'etat that toppled President Jean-Bertrand Aristide. Thousands of Haitians refugees detained at Guantanamo Bay, Cuba were deported, while Haiti was deep in political crisis.

It is estimated that 5,000-10,000 Haitians disappeared after the coup in 1991. Some were abducted and were never seen again. Others were tortured and sometimes buried alive. Young women and girls as young as 5 years old were raped by members of the FRAHP. The victims were targeted because of their political views and activities, particularly those who supported President Aristide's return.

In reaction to the US's unfair treatment, the Haitians, lacking the financial and lobbying capacity of the well established Cuban

community, took to the streets in droves to denounce the injustice of the INS's demonstrated double standard in treatment, and the abuses of the refugees' most basic rights.

According to Dr. Alex Stepick, no refugees in recent U.S. history received the bad treatment the Haitian refugees had received.

Haitian demonstrators rally to protest police brutality in a case involving the questionable death of a Haitian minister who died after being arrested on a simple traffic violation.

Under the leadership of an unassuming priest, Father Gerard Jean-Juste, and in recent years though the efforts of *Fanm Ayisyen Nan Miyami, Inc. and the Haitian-American Grassroots Coalition*, the poor Haitian refugees were successful in winning many battles.

In several lawsuits, including, *Haitian Refugee Center v. Civiletti*, in which the Court found the practice of simultaneous scheduling of Haitian cases for the purpose of deporting the refugees as fast as possible illegal, and then *Louis v. Nelson*, which approved a stipulation between INS and the Dade County Bar Association to provide representation for the Haitian boat people, and finally in *Louis v. Meissner*, which issued a preliminary injunction stopping I.N.S. from holding any exclusion hearings for the incarcerated Haitian refugees unless they have already obtained an attorney, we were able to slow down the process of immediate deportation.

In response to the Haitian Immigration Refugee Fairness Act of 1998, which was supposed to give residency to 50,000 Haitians, but didn't, and our continuing struggle against the "dry foot, wet foot policy," which underscored an overall double standard in INS treatment of the Cuban and Haitian refugees, our demonstrations grew bigger and bigger, and they attracted a wide range of supporters from the African-American leadership, Anglo, Jewish, and many other ethnic groups.

Demonstrations, rallies, sit-ins were held seven days a week, rain or shine. The ones at Krome, the INS's Detention Center on the outskirts of Miami, generated strong responses from law enforcement. They always came out in force, in riot gear, shields, batons, and horses as big as trees. Taunting us, poking and stomping on unlucky demonstrators.

We were not intimidated! We continued to come back until thousands of Haitian

Haitians of all ages turn out to demonstrate against U.S. immigration policy.

refugees were released from custody around the nation, including Peurto Rico.Many are now U.S.citizens, vying more and more to partake in the political process here in the United States. In the face of racism, discrimination, and mistreatment, the Haitian refugees showed resilience, a strong capacity to endure, and the will to survive against all odds.

Looking back now twenty years later, one can venture to say that things have improved. There are probably less Haitian refugees

in detention, however, the old is still new for hundreds of women who were transferred from Krome Avenue Detention Camp to TGK after allegations of sexual abuse by Immigration and Naturalization guards there. Instead of releasing these asylum seekers who should have not been jailed in the first place, I.N.S. sent them to a county jail that houses all kind of criminal elements where again, they were re-victimized.

Additionally, a Haitian refugee, Eddy Pierre-Paul, who claimed he had been sexually abused at the U.S. Immigration and Naturalization Service's Krome Detention Center, has been deported while his case is still under investigation. The old is still new under the I.N.S. rules for Haitian refugees. The painful, impassioned letter written by Haitian detainees from Fort Allen 20 years ago, could easily be those of the women at TGK today.

"We are asking why you treat us this way, is it because we are Negroes? Why are you letting us suffer this way, America? Don't you have a father's heart? Haven't you thought we were humans, that we had a heart to suffer with and a soul that could be wounded? Give us back our freedom. Why among all the nations that emigrate to the United States have only the Haitians known such sufferings?"

Daniel Baptiste Jr., leads Haitian protesters as they rally in front of Miami's Freedom Torch to protest against U.S. immigration policy on January 15, 2000.

ELIAN GONZALEZ

On November 25, 1999, two fishermen discovered a little boy floating in an innertube off the coast of Fort Lauderdale. That little boy was Elian Gonzalez, and his rescue not only became the stuff of legend, but prompted a struggle of wills and emotions which became a knock down, drag out battle between many in Miami's Cuban exile community and the federal government and for a while upended was passes for South Florida's sense of community.

The boy, after being released from the hospital, was paroled by the INS to his great-uncle, Lazaro Gonzalez and his family in Miami. Within days, Lazaro Gonzalez applied for asylum for Elian, against the wishes of Elian's father, Juan Miguel, who, from his home in Cuba, asked for his son to be returned to him. Elian's mother had perished in the waters off of the Florida coast sometime after placing Elian in the innertube.

On January 5, 2000, INS Commissioner Doris Meissner, informed the Miami relatives that Elian "belongs with his father," and must be returned to Cuba.

Lazaro Gonzalez responded by filing the first of many legal petitions and lawsuits in an effort to keep Elian in Miami, while members of the Cuban exile community began their own efforts by staging demonstrations, sit-in's, and a 24 hour vigil outside the home of the Elian's Miami relatives.

In the end, none of these efforts succeeded in reversing the federal government's decision to return Elian to his father. On April 22nd, in an early morning raid, INS agents, entered the home of the Elian's Miami relatives, and forcefully removed Elian, prompting a day of outrage and rioting in the streets of Miami's Cuban exile community.

On June 1st, the U.S. Court of Appeals ruled that Elian should be returned to his father, and although additional legal appeals were made to the U.S Supreme Court, Elian returned to Cuba with his father on June 28, 2000.

At a January rally protesting the INS decision to return Elian to his father, Mothers Against Repression broke through a police line, prompting thousands of exiles, gathered in downtown Miami to surge through the streets. Below, protesters march towards the Port of Miami where they staged a sit-in resulting in over 100 arrests. At right, Mireya Rubio, prays for Elian during one of several nighttime rallies for Elian in Little Havana.

On January 5, 2000, hundreds of Cuban exiles gathered in front of the home of Elian's Miami relatives in response to the news that the INS had determined that he should be returned to his father. These two little boys - neither of which is Elian - were held up in the crowd to symbolize Elian, as the crowd vowed to fight the INS decision.

Ramon Raul Sanchez, leader of the Movimiento Democracia exile group, and a supporter of non-violent protest within the exile community, was the first person to be arrested as hundreds of Cuban exiles staged a sit-down at the entrance of the Port of Miami the day after the INS ruled that Elian should be returned to his father in Cuba.

Cuban exiles had a long list of U. S. politicians and bureaucrats who they felt were in cahoots with Fidel Castro in an effort to return Elian to Cuba.

Above left, hundreds of Cuban exiles gathered in front of the home of Elian's Miami relatives almost daily for 6 months in an effort to see Elian, and provide what they believed would be a wall of bodies against any government effort to remove him by force.

Below left, a crowd gathers across from the federal courthouse in Miami as lawyers for the Gonzalez family engaged in one of the many court hearings to try and keep Elian in Miami.

Protesters at the barricade in front of Elian's Miami relatives home often provided signs for their children to wave.

Long considered hostile to the Cuban exile community by some, newspaper vending machines owned by the Miami Herald and it's latin edition, el Nuevo Herald

At one of the few occasions where Cuban exiles who opposed the return of Elian came in contact with protesters supporting his return, tempers flared and insults were hurled across the barricades.

Elza Martinez, in front of Elian's Miami relative's home, breaks into tears on the news from the U.S. Court of Appeals ordering Elian to be returned to his father in Cuba.

In the aftermath of the street protests by Cuban exiles following the INS raid on the home of Elian's Miami relatives, there was a backlash of counter-protests by many Anglos in support of Attorney General Janet Reno and her decision to seize Elian.

PROTESTS ACROSS AMERICA

THE KLU KLUX KLAN

From time to time, the Klu Klux Klan surfaces in cities around the country and manages to upset many people by announcing that they're planning to stage a rally in their city. This is usually followed by loud calls for the Klan to be denied a permit for their rally. This in turn almost always results in the ACLU stepping forward to go to court in in attempt to protect the Klan's right to free speech, again to much name calling and consternation.

In August of 1999, this drama played itself out in Cleveland, Ohio. After a period which included lawsuits, name calling and acrimony between the mayor and segments of Cleveland's Black community, the Klan was allowed to hold their rally downtown at the Cleveland Justice Center.

Attending that afternoon, were about 25 members of the Klan, about a dozen pro-Klan supporters, approximately 300 anti-Klan protesters, over 100 members of the press and over 600 Cleveland police. In a further effort to keep peace, the city erected barricades and chain link fence containment areas to keep all the factions separated.

The members of the Klan were bused into the protest area, and after an hour or so of loud music and railing at the anti Klan protesters and verbal attacks against the mayor and the police, were bussed away without incident or arrests.

Anti-Klan protesters staged a march through the city before the rally.

Members of the Nation of Islam joined the protesters.

A Cleveland police officer stands guard between the Klan and protesters.

A Klan leader attempts to address his followers above the jeers of protesters.

A protester carries a sign he hopes will be read by the Klan.

TALLAHASSEE MARCH FOR AFFIRMATIVE ACTION

On March 7, 2000, as the Florida Legislature convened on the first day of it's 2000 legislative session, over 20,000 people gathered on Tallahassee's historic Apalachee Parkway to march to the old State Capitol and rally against the decision of Governor Jeb Bush to abolish portions of Florida's affirmative action laws including those providing guidelines for entrance to Florida's state universities.

The process by which the Governor had made his decision had angered many Black Floridians, and had led to a sit-in by State Senator Kendrick Meek and State Representative Tony Hill in an effort to get the Governor's attention, and to try and persuade him to reconsider his decision.

Floridians came from all over Florida to take part in the march, and many left committed to increasing the voter participation of Black Floridians in the fall's presidential election with a campaign designated as, "Arrive With Five."

This rally and voter registration campaign was later recognized as the driving force behind the large increase in Black Floridians voting for Al Gore in the 2000 presidential election.

Above, Reverend Jesse Jackson is flanked by other Black leaders, including Florida State Senator Kendrick Meek, at left, who along with Florida State Representative Tony Hill, staged a sit-in in Governor Jeb Bush's office leading to this protest march and rally.

Right, longtime civil right leader Dick Gregory, was one of numerous civil rights leaders who attended the rally.

Far right, Reverend Jesse Jackson talks with students from Florida A & M University.

Members of Florida's NAACP gathered in the staging area before the march to the State Capitol began.

Kweisi Mfume, president of the NAACP addresses the crowd gathered at the State Capitol.

The dramatic increase in Florida's Black vote in the 2000 Presidential election had it's beginning at this demonstration.

CONFEDERATE FLAG

Throughout the South the battle to maintain the Confederate flag, or a portion of its design in state flags as a symbol of a history many do not want to forget, has led to many protests, and counter-protests, as both black and white southerners continue to wrestle with the war that divided our country over 160 years ago.

In South Carolina, a particularly virulent struggle took place over the Confederate flag flying atop the State Capitol in Columbia.

On January 8, 2000, over 6000 mostly white South Carolinians, gathered to demonstrate against the flag's removal. Many came dressed in period costumes intended to demonstrate the strong commitment to honoring their heritage as descendants of Confederate soldiers.

The protests, and threats of an economic boycott against the state continued throughout the year 2000, until the South Carolina Legislature voted to remove the flag from atop the Capitol, and have it fly as part of a Civil War Memorial on the Capitol grounds.

Gail Jeffers, dressed as a Confederate widow, was one of hundreds dressed in period costumes.

A giant Confederate flag draped across the stairs of the State Capitol in Columbia, served as a backdrop for the rally.

Supporters of the Confederate flag gathered at a local cemetery before the rally to honor Confederate veterans, then marched from the cemetery to the State Capitol.

At right, thousands of protesters brought their own Confederate flags to wave during the rally.

Ms. Alberta Martin, at 93, the last Confederate widow - she married a Confederate veteran when he was in his late 80's and she was a teenager - waves the flag from the steps of the State Capitol.

Rhea Wallace, in widow's dress, and Robert and Eddie Howlett, in Confederate uniforms, typified many who came to the rally in authentic period costume.

THE JARBIDGE SHOVEL BRIGADE

By Bob St. Louis

Near the town of Jarbidge, in northeastern Nevada, a seemingly unknown road rose to national prominence during the summer of 2000. South Canyon Road begins south of Jarbidge, and winds along the Jarbidge River, ending at the portal to the Jarbidge Wilderness Area at Snowslide Gulch The road used to continue another two miles south of Snowslide Gulch, but the Forest Service closed it in the 1970's. Jarbidge residents reopened the closed section in the 1980's, but the Forest Service placed a permanent barricade at Snowslide Gulch. The Jarbidge Wilderness Area was expanded by the Nevada Wilderness Protection Act of 1989, and the new wilderness boundary was placed at Snowslide Gulch, where the Forest Service had previously closed the road.

South Canyon Road had been established as a trail in the late 1800's by prospectors and sheepherders. By 1912, the trail had been upgraded to a road capable of handling the freight traffic supplying the mines that were being developed as part of the Jarbidge gold rush, which began with the discovery of gold ore in 1909.

In June of 1995, a major flood occurred on the Jarbidge River. The flood, characterized as a 500-year event, was produced by heavy rain falling on the snowpack. As the floodwaters rushed down the canyon, they caused considerable damage to the southernmost mile and a half of South Canyon Road. Some parts of the road were washed out, and other sections were captured by the stream, becoming the new rivercourse.

Elko County and the Forest Service had for years worked under

a cooperative maintenance agreement for South Canyon Road, which had been considered to be a county road under RS 2477. This federal statute was originally enacted as part of the Mining Law of 1866, and states: "And be it further enacted, That the right of way for the construction of highways over public lands, not reserved for other purposes, is hereby granted." One must keep in mind that a "highway" in 1866 would not equate to a present day highway. A foot trail or horse trail would have qualified as a highway, under the intent of the statute.

Both Elko County and the Forest Service began discussions leading towards repair of the road after the flood. The Forest Service volunteered to undertake the repairs, and the county honored the request. By the summer of 1997, Trout Unlimited, an organization dedicated to freshwater fish, protested the Forest Service plans to repair the road, arguing that the repair would endanger the bull trout in the river. Trout Unlimited claimed that the Jarbidge River bull trout represented the southernmost population of the fish in the United States, and deserved protection. The data supporting Trout Unlimited's claim regarding the threat to the fish are suspect, as the fish survived with the road in place for almost a century, and with mines active adjacent to the river for some 20 years. In fact, Nevada Division of Wildlife stated that the trout were present at the maximum numbers sustainable in the river.

Bob St. Louis

The Forest Service released a revised environmental assessment on June 29, 1998 that preferred replacing the road with a trail. The two previous environmental assessments had preferred repairing the road, but with threats of lawsuits from Trout Unlimited, the Forest Service felt a trail would be better. On July 2 the Forest Service met with Jarbidge residents to inform them that the road would not be repaired. The Forest Service did not hold scoping meetings, or discuss the change in plans with the Elko County Commission.

On July 15, 1998, the Commission passed Elko County

Ordinance 74-98. The ordinance declared an emergency condition, due to the imminent threat of catastrophic fire in the South Canyon. Six days later, on July 21, 1998, Elko County road crews began to repair the road. Simultaneously, the United States Fish and Wildlife Service held hearings in Jackpot, Nevada, regarding the "agency" proposed listing of the bull trout as a threatened species.

The Corps of Engineers issued a cease and desist order against Elko County on July 23, 1998, for alleged violations of the Clean Water Act. Elko County Road Supervisor Otis Tipton flatly denied that county crews had worked in the river.

On August 1, 1998, the Fish and Wildlife Service issued an emergency listing of the Jarbidge River bull trout under the Endangered Species Act, even though the Nevada Division of Wildlife objected to the listing.

The Environmental Protection Agency gave the Forest Service permission to "stabilize" the section of the road that Elko County had begun to repair. The Forest Service hired an engineering firm, through a sole-source contract, to oversee the work. In mid-November, the "stabilization" work was begun, which included cutting down numerous trees, piling tons of debris at the down-canyon end of the road, and placing three large boulders as a barricade. Over $400,000 was spent by the Forest Service doing the so-called "stabilization" work. To put this in perspective, it typically costs about one mil-

lion dollars to build one mile of paved two-lane highway, or $200 per lineal foot; the Forest Service spent $400 per lineal foot "stabilizing 1,000 feet of a dirt road.

Elko County was indignant at this clearly unwarranted action taken by a federal agency on a county road. Adding further to the County's frustration, on March 30, 1999, the Nevada Division of Wildlife released a report that clearly stated that "the Jarbidge bull trout population is neither threatened nor endangered." This report had some impact, as the Fish and Wildlife Service then reduced the status of the trout from endangered to threatened.

On August 30, 1999, the United States notified Elko County that it would be required to repay the United States for the costs incurred in the "stabilization" effort, and that fines for violation of the Clean Water Act had been accumulating since the previous summer.

One of the trucks that carried the shovels to Jarbidge.

In September 1999, Assemblyman John Carpenter, attorney Grant Gerber, and Elko businessman O.Q. "Chris" Johnson informed the Elko County Commission that they were forming a citizens "work party to repair the road, using man and horse power. Nevada's Attorney General, Frankie Sue Del Papa, warned Elko County District Attorney Gary Woodbury, that her office would take legal action against anyone working on the road.

On October 7, 1999, U.S. District Judge David Hagen issued a restraining order against the so-called road rebels. Nonetheless, hundreds of supporters gathered in Jarbidge on October 9 to demonstrate their resolve, although they did not engage in any roadwork. Two weeks later the Elko County Commission convened an evidentiary hearing into the validity of the County's claim to ownership of the road. Five days later Judge Hagen joined Elko County in the case that was being pleaded against the road rebels, Carpenter, Johnson, and Gerber.

Gloria Flora, who was then Supervisor of the Humboldt-Toiyabe National Forest, resigned her position on November 8, 1999, with the resignation effective on January 1, 2000. She cited the "rampant anti-federal" sentiment in Nevada, and alleged that Forest Service employees had been mistreated, and even threatened, in Elko county. Assemblyman Carpenter, and the U.S. Attorney for Nevada, Kathryn Landreth, both investigated her claims, and found them unfounded.

On November 13, 1999, Congressmen Jim Gibbons (Nevada) and Helen Chenoweth-Hage (Idaho) convened a field hearing on the South Canyon Road dispute. The Forest Service refused to cooperate during the hearing. In fact, the House Resources Committee finally had to subpoena Forest Service Chief Mike Dombeck in order to obtain all the evidence and testimony required for the investigation.

In December 1999, a group of Elko county residents, including Demar Dahl, Elwood Mose, James Muth, and Mel Steninger peti-

tioned the court to join the three road rebels in the case. Judge Hagen denied this request in January 2000. When Judge Hagen announced his decision, Demar Dahl stated that he would lead a work party to the road on July 4, 2000, to reopen it.

On January 3, 2000, Eureka, Montana sawmill owner Jim Hurst began to organize the "Shovels of Solidarity," with the goal of shipping 10,000 shovels to Elko as a show of support for the road rebels. Hurst and other logging business owners had been hurt financially by Forest Servicepolicies in Montana, and were anxious to help the Elko county group fight back.

A 30-foot tall shovel was erected on the Elko County Courthouse lawn on January 20, 2000. The shovel was built by the Elko Blacksmith Shop, and was paid for by John Carpenter. For one dollar, a donor could have their name placed on the shovel. In less than a week, over 2,000 names were on the shovel. Within a year, a sideboard had to be added to accommodate over 8,000 names. The shovel would suffer acts of vandalism during its first year on display; most Elkoans ascribed these acts of vandalism to environmental extremists. Picnic tables, symbolizing the family values of access to federally managed lands, also began to arrive in Elko. Like the shovel, some of the picnic tables also suffered acts of vandalism.

The largest parade in Elko history heralded the arrival of some 10,000 shovels from Montana on January 29, 2000. Many of the

Volunteers clear rocks before people with shovels came in to level the road.

shovels bore the names and hometowns of the people that had donated them. States represented included Montana, Idaho, Oregon, Washington, Wyoming, and Utah. The parade down Elko's main thoroughfare, Idaho Street, had some 5,000 participants.

On March 13, 2000, Demar Dahl formed the Jarbidge Shovel Brigade, with the intention of raising the funds necessary to stage the road reopening in July. Besides desiring to reopen the road, the Brigade stated its intent to help Elko County affirm its RS 2477 right of way to the road. On April 13, 2000, Elko County Commissioners donated the 10,000 shovels to the Shovel Brigade.

On November 23, 1999, Judge Hagen had ordered Elko County, the three road rebels, and the United States into mediation. The mediation began March 8, and concluded on June 20, 2000, after more than 100 hours of discussion. The agreement forged during the mediation process was released to the public, and a Special County Commission meeting was held on June 28 to hear public comment. All parties to the mediation gave presentations on their positions with respect to the agreement. The United States' representatives all hailed the agreement as a win-win. John Carpenter was not happy with the deal, but indicated he might sign it. Grant Gerber was fierce in his criticism of the document, noting that it gave everything to the United States, and because of this, he would not even allow his name to be placed on the document. O.Q."Chris" Johnson also

Everyone took turns as part of the Shovel Brigade.

indicated that he would not sign it, for reasons similar to Gerber's.

Commissioners' Tony Lesperance, Nolan Lloyd, and Brad Roberts were strongly opposed to signing. Commissioner Mike Nannini, who had been one of the county representatives in mediation, felt the agreement was fair. Commission Chairwoman Roberta Skelton, who had also sat in mediation, leaned toward not accepting the deal.

Public comments were, with one exception, strongly against signing the agreement. Most of the public speakers blasted the deal, claiming that it gave the United States way more than it was entitled to. During the public comment period, Demar Dahl announced that the Justice Department had that afternoon served him with papers requesting an emergency restraining order against the Shovel Brigade. A teleconference hearing was held the following day, before U.S. District Judge Philip Pro. Pro denied the restraining order request, noting that as long as the Brigade did not violate the Clean Water or Endangered Species Acts, the planned protest could proceed.

On July 3, 2000, the first busload of Brigade supporters arrived at South Canyon Road from the staging camp established in Three Creek, Idaho, some 30 miles away. By noon on July 4, hundreds of volunteers had repaired the "stabilized" section of the road to a degree that allowed a pickup truck to be driven over it.

Prior to the event, the Shovel Brigade had hired a consulting engineer to lay out the area that could be legally worked on, so that the Clean Water and Endangered Species Acts would not be violated.

People worked on the road with such enthusiasm that more than twice the work could have been accomplished had the Brigade not honored its self-imposed limits. In fact, people were somewhat dismayed when they were told that their "shift" was over, and it was time for the next crew to work on the road.

While the roadwork was going on, a " bucket brigade" had walked to one of the Forest Service out-houses that were up the closed road. They removed the waste from the vault beneath the out-house, put it in buckets, which were sealed and carried back to the barricade area.

When the roadwork was completed and the bucket brigade had returned, the crowd, numbering almost 1,000, gathered at the three large boulders blocking the road. John Carpenter, Elwood Mose, and Commissioner Nolan Lloyd all gave brief speeches. Suzanne Jusst, from Twin Falls, Idaho, sang the " road song" that she had written, and the crowd sang the " Star Spangled Banner" after reciting the Pledge of Allegiance. Chains and ropes had been attached to the center rock, which had been dubbed " Liberty Rock." With Demar Dahl leading the group, hundreds of people pulled the rock out of the way, completing the opening.

The event was peaceful, no one was injured, and no arrests were made. Everyone present agreed that it was a very successful

A bagpiper arrived to rally the members of the Brigade as they cleared the road.

protest. However, on August 4, 2000, the Justice Department filed a complaint against the Shovel Brigade and Demar Dahl, alleging that the Brigade had trespassed during the protest. Then, on August 17, 2000, the United States announced it was lifting the stay on the lawsuit against the road rebels and Elko County, and requested authorization from the court to close the road again.

During the fall of 2000 several prominent legal authorities, including the Legislative Counsel Bureau of Nevada, and attorneys John Howard (from San Diego, California) and Carla Boucher (from Chesapeake, Virginia) were received in Elko. All of them advised against signing the clearly one-sided mediation agreement. Also received was Helen Chenoweth Hage's, Chairwoman's Report to the Subcommittee on Forests and Forest Health.

The Congresswoman was blunt in her appraisal of the actions taken by the Forest Service on the road, and clearly concluded that the agency was well outside its legal rights to do what it had done.

In October 2000, Elko construction company owner Mike Lattin organized the Citizens Road Repair Committee, which comprised a group of engineers and scientists who would work on an environmentally friendly method of repairing the road. The committee worked on plans throughout the winter, and hoped to begin work on the road in July 2001.

On November 2, 2000, Judge Hagen ruled against the Justice Department's motion to re-close the road, and ordered the parties back into mediation. On November 8, 2000, the Elko County Commission voted four to one to reject the original mediation proposal that had been presented in June 2000; Mike Nannini cast the sole opposing vote, arguing that the County could not afford a lengthy legal battle with the federal government.

Court-sponsored mediation in the Elko County/road rebel case began on January 17, 2001, in Magistrate Judge Robert McQuaid's Reno court. Grant Gerber, who not only represented himself in the Elko County/road rebel case, but also acted as counsel for Dahl and the Shovel Brigade, had tried unsuccessfully to get the Brigade case joined with the other case. By February 16, 20001, a new agreement had been brokered. While it appeared to be very similar to the original mediation agreement, it contained a key element that was missing from the first agreement: the United States recognized "Elko County" RS 2477 right of way (the original agreement would have given the county an administrative right of way, which could be revoked by a Forest Service administrator

The Demar Dahl and Shovel Brigade case entered court-spon-

sored mediation on March 5, 2000. After a very long day of negotiations, the Brigade case was apparently settled, with the Brigade agreeing to do no work in South Canyon without Elko County approval; that approval would have to be approved by the Forest Service, per the Elko County settlement agreement.

Everything appeared to be heading to conclusion, when an Associated Press article published on March 22, 2001, quoted Bob Williams, Field Supervisor for the Nevada Fish and Wildlife Service, as saying he doubted the road would ever be repaired. Comments Williams made in the article infuriated Brigade supporters, who felt that Williams was being "predecisional" and had negotiated the settlement in bad faith.

On April 2, 2001, Judge McQuaid held teleconferences to determine if the two cases were going to close. The first teleconference concerned the Elko County/road rebels case; everyone on both sides agreed that they would sign the agreement, except for Grant Gerber and "Chris" Johnson. Gerber's reasons for not signing were largely because the case against the Brigade was not yet done, and he felt that signing would possibly leave the Brigade out to dry. Johnson refused to sign because

The bolder called " Liberty" is moved by members of the Brigade.

he felt he and the County had done nothing wrong, so he was not going to sign.

The second teleconference was conducted to see if the Brigade case was going to be finished. Demar Dahl told Judge McQuaid that the comments made by Bob Williams in the earlier newspaper article had the Brigade convinced that Williams had negotiated in bad faith, and as a result, the Brigade wanted language added to the agreement stipulating that as long as the road remained open, the Brigade would not work in the canyon without Elko County approval. The judge, and U.S. Attorney Blaine Welsh, both stated that Williams had not spoken with full agency authority, and therefore his comments were meaningless. Dahl pressed the issue, which caused the judge to immediately set a discovery schedule leading to trial.

Helen Wilson, at 90, Jarbidge's oldest citizen, rides across the newly opened road.

After the teleconference, Grant Gerber spoke with Blaine Welsh, who assured Gerber that Williams did not speak with full agency authority when he made his comments to the press. Gerber discussed Welsh's comments with the Shovel Brigade board of trustees, who decided to accept the agreement as written. The long battle was over, at least for the time being.

The Shovel Brigade hailed both agreements as victories, and noted that the two reasons that the Brigade had organized, to open the road and to secure the "County" RS 2477 right of way, had been realized. The barely one year old grassroots organization from a sparsely populated Nevada county, with the support of people throughout the West, and as far away as Rhode Island and Tasmania, had taken on the federal government and won.

What separates the Shovel Brigade's protest from most derives from two key elements: Firstly, the Brigade enlisted people to actually do something, on the ground, to address a wrong committed by the United States. Secondly, strong leadership from Assemblyman John Carpenter and most of the Elko County Commission enabled the cause to quickly grow and become a force to be reckoned with. In the end, Jarbidge showed that the resolve of principled Americans can still defeat oppression, and by hanging tough, the common people can take the government to task.

REDEEM THE DREAM

Thirty seven years after the historic March on Washington D.C., and the delivery by Martin Luther King of his famous, "I Have A Dream," speech, his son, Martin Luther King III, and the Reverend Al Sharpton, staged the **Redeem The Dream** rally on the steps of the Lincoln Memorial to call attention to the problems of racial profiling and police brutality.

"My father stood not far from here, trying to redeem the soul of America. I challenge you to ensure that he did not die in vain." King's son told the crowd.

The practice of racial profiling by police departments across the country has become a critical issue for civil rights leaders who met with President Clinton the day before the Rally to call on him to issue an executive order that would ban the practice.

Speakers, including Abner Louima, who was attacked in the bathroom of a New York police station and the mother of Amadou Diallo, called for a stronger federal involvement in investigating her son's death at the hands of four policemen who fired 41 bullets after claiming they mistook Diallo's wallet for a gun.

Approximately 50,000 people attend the rally, which also included speeches by Dick Gregory, Don King, Malik Shabazz of the New Black Panther Party and Benjamin Mohammed of the Nation Of Islam.

A young boy looks for friends in the crowd.

Don King, Kweisi Mfume, president of the NAACP, and New York civil rights lawyer Sanford Rubenstein before the rally.

At right, some of the 50,000 plus who attended the rally gathered on both sides of the Reflecting Pool.

Below left and right, the fist of defiance and the out-stretched hand of prayer represented the divergence of reactions to the call of speakers to stand up in opposition to racial profiling and getting out the vote.

Coretta Scott King, flanked by Reverend Walter Fauntroy and Reverend Al Sharpton, is escorted to the podium to speak.

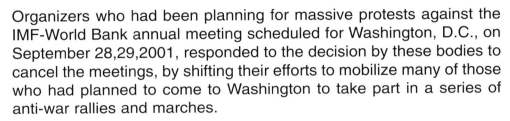

GIVE PEACE A CHANCE

The peace movement in America was quick to mobilize in the aftermath of the September 11th attacks on New York's World Trade Center and the Pentagon in Washington, D.C..

Organizers who had been planning for massive protests against the IMF-World Bank annual meeting scheduled for Washington, D.C., on September 28,29,2001, responded to the decision by these bodies to cancel the meetings, by shifting their efforts to mobilize many of those who had planned to come to Washington to take part in a series of anti-war rallies and marches.

On Saturday morning, September 28th, the *Anti-Capitalist Bloc*, staged a march with approximately 1000 participants from the U.S. Capitol grounds to the World Bank headquarters.

On Saturday afternoon, the *International Action Center* organized a rally at Freedom Plaza which attracted approximately 7500 demonstrators who then marched down Pennsylvania Avenue to the U.S. Capitol. Along the way they were challenged by approximately 150 counter-protesters.

On Sunday, September 29th, the *Washington Peace Center* organized a rally at Washington's Malcolm X Park, which attracted approximately 3000 demonstrators, who then marched through N.W. Washington, stopping for another rally at Sheridan Park, across from the Turkish Embassy, where a small group of Kurdish refugees have been staging a protest against the Turkish treatment of the Kurds.

Protests also took place across America at over 130 college campuses in the days after the attacks and then tapered off.

After marching the length of Pennsylvania Avenue on Saturday, protesters gathered on the Capitol grounds for a rally.

Sunday's protesters gathered behind this banner before setting off for a march through N.W. Washington.

President George W. Bush and his policies were the focus of many protesters during the weekend's marches and rallies.

Counter protesters gathered on Pennsylvania Avenue to express their thoughts about the peace marchers.

COURAGE OF THEIR CONVICTIONS

THE COURAGE OF THEIR CONVICTIONS

What prompts an individual to protest? As demonstrated in this book, there are any number of social or political issues which can prompt hundreds, thousands, or even tens of thousands of people to come together in an effort to bring attention or raise opposition to an issue. However, it's that lone protester, often with a quixotic message - like Frank Chu, at right, marching through the streets of San Francisco on a weekday afternoon - that gains our attention in a way that crowds of protesters often don't.

The following individuals stood out as exemplifying the uniqueness of individual protest during my travels for this project. Several, part of large demonstrations stood out for their willingness to state their opinion in a unique way. Others were individuals espousing unpopular or unsettling opinions. Others just had a message that was uniquely personal.

All of them however, had one thing in common; a willingness to stand up and say what they believed, even if in doing so they incurred the laughter or wrath of those they sought to persuade.

David Roy Bradt, a regular at Venice Beach in Los Angeles, shows his aversion to circumcision, which he says is a sore point with him.

David Caso, a member of the group Free Republic, along with other members of that group, staged weekly Saturday protests outside the White House during the last 20 months of President Clinton's term in office.

A member of the Seattle Lesbian Avengers, marching at the WTO uses her body to comment on her opposition to the use of Tampons

Lou Santucci, at right, engages in a one man counter-demonstration against Peace marchers in Washington, D.C., shortly after the September 11th, attacks.

MARIAH

By Nate Madsen

What is it like to live in an ancient redwood? It is to have the most glorious view of the splendor of creation all around, and it is to have a disgusting view of how that creation is disrespected; clear-cut forests, barren hillsides, landslides and debris torrents that result from industrial logging operations.

The forest has more beauty than words can convey, and industrial logging has a face uglier than the devil himself. It was a mixed bag full of passion for life, and sadness for the loss of such sacred forests, and a true blessing of contemplation. For once there was time enough to think.

Different conclusions seem appropriate when frantic business doesn't monopolize the day. I definitely consider logging honorable work and have found loggers to generally be kind-hearted, tough shelled, family oriented, and hard working, good people. They have a rowdy element which is bad if you're a tree protector and receive a nasty beating or worse, but generally I like loggers, and I like the idea of logging with respect for the land as a primary focus.

That is one of the many reasons I climbed Mariah, the tree I called home for 2 years. I want to see logging honored for what it provides. Unfortunately, the rate and scale at which it is currently performed must be drastically reduced to ensure a functioning forest ecology system that will be capable of supporting dependent species and provide wooden products far into the distant future.

I love wood and I love trees. I love loggers and I love protesters. There is no conflict in this passion I feel for both sides. Without wood homes, protesters would be wet and miserable all of the time instead of most of the time. It is tough work, protecting these forests. Wet cold nights are a given, and people endure those nights with love and grace. I know because I've had my share.

Nate Madsen, on a lower branch 80 feet up in Mariah.

The same goes for loggers. It is often cold, wet and miserable in the rain forest, whether you carry a banner or a chainsaw. As protesters need wood, loggers need trees. Where would a logger be without trees? FIRED! The difference between timber workers and tree protectors are simply the clothes we wear, the foods we eat, and the tools we use to do our work. Other then that we are basically the same. We all want there to be trees forever and wood forever. What keeps us from working together is a large, thick, sharp piercing wedge that drives us apart. Every public relations campaign scam, every heated headline, and slanderous comment that pushes our common goal farther into the realm of conflict by magnifying the details that differ, rather than accepting our mutual needs, and working in concert rather than in chaos.

We must somehow, find ways to overcome the differences. Until we do however, people like me who love our old growth forests will continue to climb these trees and use our bodies as shields against their destruction. **WE OWE IT TO FUTURE GENERATIONS.**

Concepcion "Connie" Picciotto, has been protesting for world peace and against the proliferation of weapons of mass destruction in Lafayette Park, across from the White House since August 1981. Her staying powers have frustrated Washington bureaucrats and police over the years who have engaged in numerous schemes in an effort to evict her.

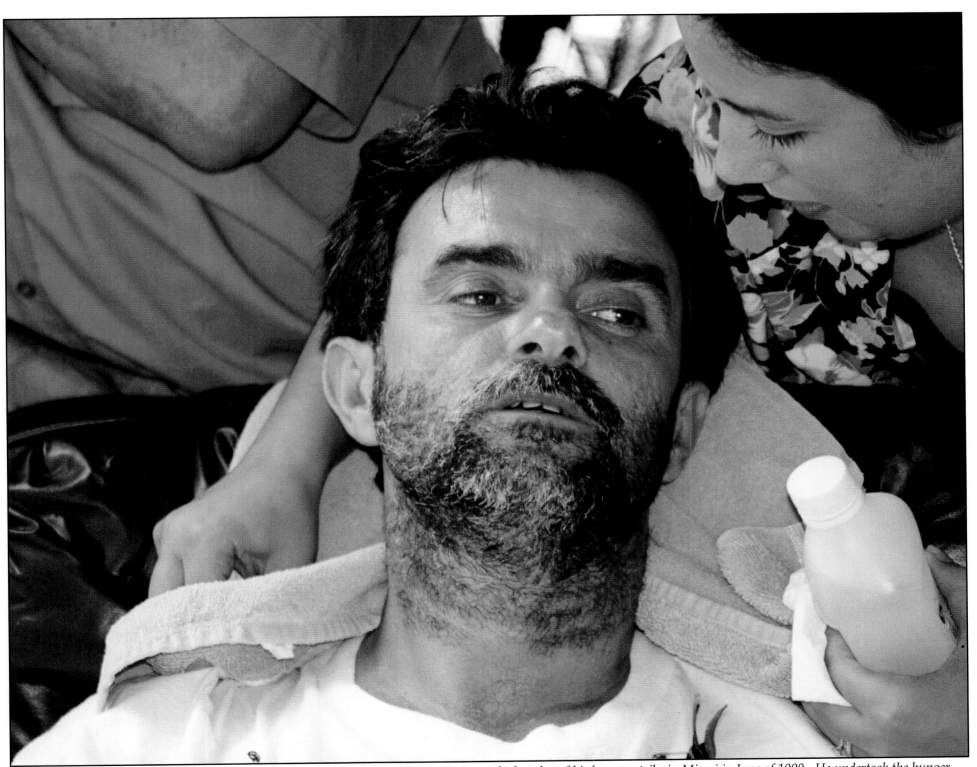

Ramon Raul Sanchez, a leader of the Cuban exile group, Movimiento Democracia, on the last day of his hunger strike in Miami in June of 1999. He undertook the hunger strike to protest the federal government's seizure of his boat before he could take off to Cuba on a protest mission. After 20 days, he ended his strike when the government agreed to return his boat.

This woman draws attention to her sexual orientation outside the 2000 Southern Baptist Convention, in Orlando.

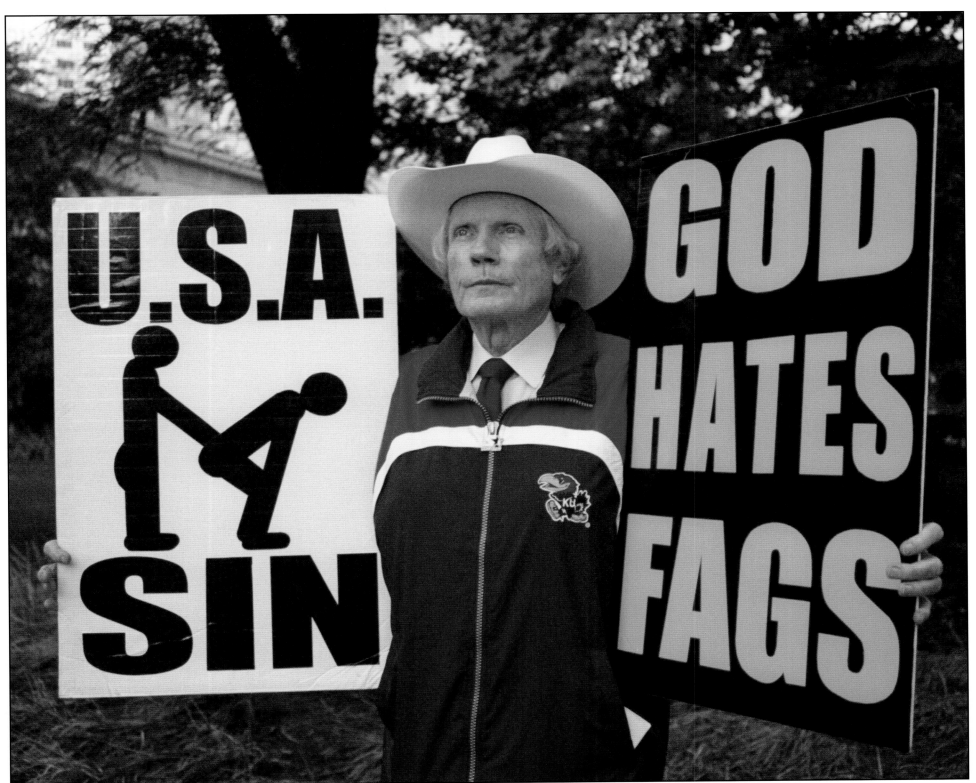

The Reverend Donald Phelps, of Wichita, Kansas, outside the Ohio State Capitol, in August 1999, offers his opinion on homosexuality.

ESSAY WRITERS

NICOLAS BARRICADA is an anarchist and the founder of the Barricada Collective.

MARLEINE BASTIEN is the founder, former president, and current Executive Director of Fanm Ayisyen Nan Miyami, Inc. (Haitian Women of Miami, founded in 1991. This organization helps Haitian women by offering a wide variety of resources, including immigration and advocacy, breast cancer education and outreach, women workers empowerment, education welfare, family intervention, empowerment, and education. She is one of the founders of the Haitian-American Grassroots Coalition and also formed the "Justice Coalition for the Haitian Children of Guantanamo. In 2000 she received the "Human Right Award" from Amnesty International and the "MS Women of the Year Award"in December of 2001.

FATHER ROY BOURGEOIS is a decorated Naval Officer who served in Vietnam. Following his discharge he became a Catholic priest in the Maryknoll Missionary Order. While working with the poor in Bolivia he was arrested and forced to leave the country. In 1980, he became involved in El Salvador after two friends were part of the four U. S. churchwomen raped and killed by Salvadorian soldiers. This and similar acts led him to become an outspoken critic of U.S. foreign policy in Latin America, and led to his founding the School of The Americas (SOA) Watch in 1990. Since then he has spent over 4 years in federal prisons for non-violent protests against the training of Latin American soldiers at Ft. Benning, Georgia. In 1997 he was the recipient of the Pax Christi USA Teacher Of Peace Award. He also received an Academy Award nomination for his1983 documentary film, "Gods Of Metal."

ADAM EIDINGER is a Washington, DC based social justice activist. As a founding member of the Mintwood Media Collective, a worker owned and operated public relations firm, he has spearheaded many effective public events ranging from anti-corporate globalization protests to medical marijuana. He is a frequent spokesperson for change and is active with the DC Statehood Green Party and the Mobilization for the Global Justice. Adam is 28 years old.

BRUCE FRIEDRICH is Director of Vegan Outreach for People for the Ethical Treatment of Animals (PETA). He can be found speaking at schools, meeting with civic clubs, debating meat industry officials on television, or streaking the queen of England with "www.GoVeg.com" painted on his back.

NATHAN MADSEN is a Northern California forest advocate, climbed a 1000 year old redwood named Mariah and lived in her branches for 2 years to protect her from the chain saws of the debt driven MAXXAM/Pacific Lumber. Nate also works as a tree planter and has planted 100,000 trees and counting since returning to the ground in an effort to help bridge the gap between timber workers and environmental enthusiasts by trying to leave a brighter tomorrow through our actions today.

JOHN SELLERS is the director of the Ruckus Society where he provides political vision and teaches a variety of workshops. For six years during the nineties, he worked with Greenpeace coordinating dozens of actions throughout the US. In 1995 he sailed with the SV Rainbow Warrior in the North Atlantic and Mediterranean to halt drift net fishing. In the last six years he has traveled extensively throughout North America coordinating direct actions for Rainforest Action Network, Earth First!, Project Underground, International Campaign for Tibet, Global Exchange, The United Steel Workers of America and many others. In June of 2000 he was permanently removed from Canada (his favorite country in North America).

BOB ST. LOUIS joined the Jarbidge Shovel Brigade as a volunteer helping raise funds for the road opening that took place in July 2000. He is credited with finding the key piece of evidence proving Elko County's rightful title to the road, and presented that evidence in U.S. District Court. He became president of the Brigade in 2001, and led a convoy to Klamath Falls in August 2001 to support the Klamath Basin farmers. He also serves on the Elko County Public Land Use Advisory Commission.

WITH SPECIAL THANKS TO

Bob Presner
Phil Sandlin
Brad Davis
Jon Ward
Rick Bowmer
Randy Limpkin
Courtney Sage
Andres Bruetsch
Carl Hersh
Kathy Hersh
Katie Hersh
Fabian Scheffold
Istvan Vizner
Diane Williams
Jeorg Birker
Laura Jaffee
Jamin O'Brien

William J. McCarthy, my QuarkExpress wizard
Elizabeth Bryan, my queen of print making

Thanks also to the ACLU of Southern California and attornies Michael Small and Peter Eliasberg,

&

MILBANK, TWEED, HADLEY & McCLOY LLP
Michael Diamond   Chandra Gooding
Sharon Jackson   Ken Ostrow
Julie A. Kaplan

for taking on the lawsuit *Al Crespo, et al, vs The City of Los Angeles et al*, which resulted in the LA Police Department agreeing to change their policies and procedures in dealing with the press during times of crisis and civil unrest, thereby reducing the possibility of the press being shot at or beaten while doing their job.

Canon cameras and lenses were used on this project
Kodak film was used on this project
QuarkExpress was used in the book's layout

The typeface Palatino was used for the text in this book.
The typeface Garage Shock was used for the headers in this book

SECTIONS/PHOTO IDENTIFICATION

WHO'S VOTE? OUR VOTE: Protesters take a time out at Democratic Convention in Los Angeles.

THIS IS WHAT DEMOCRACY LOOKS LIKE: Protesters with sign on bedsheet march in Washington, D.C., during the 2000 IMF/World Bank protests.

LIFE AND DEATH: A lone protester lies in the street in front at Fort Benning, Georgia, during the annual SOA Watch protest in 2000, as part of a street action to symbolize the murder of peasants in Columbis and Boliva.

EXILES AT THE BARRICADES: Cuban exiles protest in front of the Biltimore Hotel in Coral Gables in 1999.

PROTESTS ACROSS AMERICA: A protester is arrested by military police at Vandenburg Airforce Base protesting the continuing decision of the Bush administration to go forward with the "Star Wars" missile defense program.

COURAGE OF CONVICTIONS: A protester in New York City at the annual anti-police brutality rally held annually on October 22nd.

Photo of Bob St. Louis on page 154: Terry St. Louis